Election
2004

Election 2004

HOW BUSH WON AND WHAT YOU CAN EXPECT IN THE FUTURE

Evan Thomas

WITH REPORTING BY
Eleanor Clift, Kevin Peraino,
Jonathan Darman, Peter Goldman,
Holly Bailey, and Suzanne Smalley

PublicAffairs
New York

Copyright © 2004 by Newsweek, Inc.

Published in the United States by PublicAffairs™,
a member of the Perseus Books Group.

All rights reserved.
Printed in the United States of America.

No part of this book may be reproduced in any manner whatsoever without
written permission except in the case of brief quotations embodied in critical
articles and reviews. For information, address PublicAffairs, 250 West 57th Street,
Suite 1321, New York, NY 10107. PublicAffairs books are available at special
discounts for bulk purchases in the U.S. by corporations, institutions, and other
organizations. For more information, please contact the Special Markets
Department at the Perseus Books Group, 11 Cambridge Center, Cambridge,
MA 02142, call (617) 252-5298, or email special.markets@perseusbooks.com.

Book design by Jane Raese

ISBN 1-58648-293-9

FIRST EDITION

2 4 6 8 10 9 7 5 3 1

CONTENTS

Sen. John Kerry on his campaign bus, February 15, 2004, as he heads to a rally in Green Bay, Wisconsin. Behind him (middle) is his press secretary David Wade and senior political advisor Bob Shrum. Kerry narrowly won the Wisconsin primary. (Photo by David Hume Kennerly/Getty Images for *Newsweek*)

Presidential candidate Howard Dean campaigns in Ames, Iowa, while travelling through the state on the afternoon of the Iowa caucus, January 19, 2004

Karen Hughes, White House Press Secretary Scott McClellan and White House senior adviser Karl Rove on Air Force One between Farmington and Albuquerque, New Mexico (Photo by Charles Ommanney/contact for *Newsweek*)

Sen. John Kerry and his wife Teresa Heinz Kerry share a private moment before taking the stage and declaring victory, January 27, 2004, in the New Hampshire primary

President George W. Bush visits Fort Polk Army Post near Leesville, Louisiana, to address members of the U.S. Army, including a large contingent of Army National Guard and family members, February 17, 2004

Democratic presidential candidate John Kerry campaigns on Independence Day during a rainstorm with his two daughters Vanessa and Alex (right), in Cedar Rapids, Iowa, July 4, 2004

(Photo by David Hume Kennerly/Getty Images for *Newsweek*)

Veterans salute John Kerry as he arrives in Dayton, Ohio, on July 7, 2004, with his wife, Teresa Heinz Kerry

(Photo by David Hume Kennerly / Getty Images for *Newsweek*)

Kerry and Edwards in Ft. Lauderdale, Florida, July 8, 2004
(Photo by David Hume Kennerly / Getty Images for *Newsweek*)

President Bush meeting with his defense team at his ranch in Crawford, Texas, August 23, 2004 (foreground left to right Andy Card, Condi Rice, Donald Rumsfeld and President Bush)

(Photo by Charles Ommanney/Contact for *Newsweek*)

Members of Kerry's "War Room" watch as Sen. John Kerry and President George W. Bush participate in their final debate, Wednesday, October 13, 2004, in Phoenix, Arizona (Photo by Khue Bui for *Newsweek*)

President George W. Bush speaks at a Victory 04 rally in Manchester, New Hampshire. At his side is First Lady Laura Bush, October 29, 2004

(Photo by Charles Ommanney / Contact for *Newsweek*)

Senior adviser Karl Rove and the Bush team work through the night in the old family dinning room of the White House as the results come in, November 2, 2004 (Photo by Charles Ommanney/Contact for *Newsweek*)

How Bush Did It

A team of Newsweek *reporters unveils the
untold fears, secret battles and private emotions
behind a historic election.*

I N THE WINTER OF 2003–04, Jenna Bush, one of President Bush's 22-year-old twin daughters, dreamed that her father lost the election. Jenna had never before shown any interest in politics or much desire to get involved in her father's campaigns. But now she, along with her sister, Barbara, volunteered to help their father get re-elected. The president was overjoyed to have the girls on the campaign bus, recalled his wife, Laura. His mood lightened, to the relief of his handlers, who had been anxiously discussing their candidate's surliness and impatience.

Politics has been a family business, and a family war, since long before the Capulets and Montagues began plotting against each other. Alexandra Kerry, the Democratic nominee's 31-year-old daughter, disliked politics, but she campaigned hard for her father anyway, until one day hecklers called her a "baby killer." Weeping in her father's arms, she confessed her fear that the Republicans would steal the election. Kerry comforted her, telling her that he would not let that happen (just in case, his campaign recruited 10,000 lawyers).

For all the billions spent and the efforts to make elections a semi-science (Karl Rove, Bush's chief adviser, was always studying "metric mileposts" in his get-out-the-vote operation), politics is intensely personal. Presidential candidates are in some ways objects, screens upon which we project hopes and dreams, fears and hatreds. But they are also human—they are husbands and fathers, they have insecurities and doubts, moments of loneliness and fatigue. They are motivated to run for office by visions of a better country but also by old resentments and angers. This was especially true in the 2004 presidential election.

It is not clear when George W. Bush and John Kerry first met. Kerry once recalled Bush, none too fondly, to writer Julia Reed of *Vogue* magazine: "He was two years behind me at Yale, and I knew him, and he's still the same guy." Bush says he has no recollection of meeting Kerry at Yale. Both presidential candidates were members of the same college secret society, Skull and Bones, but brothers they were not. The two men had disliked each other before they knew each other.

Bush did not remember Kerry but he knew the type: sanctimonious suck-ups who looked down on fun-loving fellows like George W. Bush. In the world according to Bush, guys like

Kerry were not out just to ruin Yale. They wanted to take over the whole country, to impose the smug, know-it-all liberal ideology on regular, God-fearing, hardworking Americans. Kerry's regard for Bush was just as dismissive. Kerry may or may not have met Bush at Yale but he had met his kind before. At Kerry's prep school, boys like Bush were known as "regs," regular guys, the cool, sarcastic in-crowd that made awkward, too-eager-to-please boys like John F. Kerry feel low and left out. The regs were insular, stuck up, too sure of themselves to reach out to, or even see, the wider world.

It is impossible to understand the 2004 presidential campaign without appreciating the nature of the animus between the two men. It wasn't entirely personal; the candidates were capable of saying gracious things about each other's family. But their differences went beyond party or ideology or styles of leadership. Each saw the other as a symbol of the wrong side of the great post-1960s divide. Bush eyed Kerry and saw the worst of Blue State America—a pseudo-intellectual, a Frenchified phony, a dithering weakling. Rove built a whole campaign around this point of view, casting Kerry as a "flip-flopper," "out of the mainstream," clinging to the effete "left bank" of society. Kerry looked down on Bush and saw the worst of Red State America, a know-nothing who blustered and swaggered, even though his head was stuck in the sand. The two candidates could debate lofty issues in a time of war, but their mutual disdain showed through.

Thanks to modern technology and the influence of money, Bush and Kerry could summon enormous resources to bash each other. The 2004 presidential campaign was the first $1 billion–plus campaign (up from roughly $600 million in 2000). About the only good thing that can be said about the cascade of money, much of it from special interests, flowing into the campaign was that it was probably a wash—a zero-sum game, a case of massive overkill on both sides. Both Kerry and Bush were able to call on some very clever political minds. Indeed, Kerry could not stop calling on them—he used his cell phone so much that his handlers twice took it away. Kerry's tendency to endlessly revisit decisions muddled his message. Often, he seemed so tangled up in dependent clauses that he lost sight of the larger issues facing the country.

KERRY (LIKE BUSH) is a far more complex man than the caricature he helped create. He could be decent, thoughtful, sensitive, especially with his well-loved daughters, Alexandra and Vanessa. He had proved his toughness and resilience in war and politics; he was a searching and careful thinker. And yet at times he seemed like a shallow opportunist with a finger in the air. Politicians, of course, need both vision and practicality to get anything accomplished, and Kerry, while often cautious, could also be bold. Both to heal the bitter partisan divide and because he would do anything to win, Kerry offered to make GOP Sen. John McCain a kind of grand national-security czar—serving as both secretary of Defense and vice president in a Kerry administration. McCain declined and supported Bush.

In an interview with two *Newsweek* reporters aboard Air Force One in August, Bush was funny and relaxed, self-confident enough to be self-effacing. He is blessed with a patient and caring wife who can tell him when he has gone too far. Yet the peevishness that he showed in the first presidential debate was never too far from the surface. Bush may believe in himself too much. Or, more precisely, perhaps, he has banished his self-doubt to the point where he mistakes his own ego for the national purpose.

For more than a year, *Newsweek* followed the presidential campaigns of both men from the inside. Beginning in mid-2003, a team of *Newsweek* reporters detached from the weekly magazine to devote themselves to observing, recording and shaping the narrative that follows. The reporters were granted unusual access to the staffs and families of both candidates on the understanding that the information they learned would not be made public until the magazine's special election issue—after the votes were cast on Nov. 2.

Viewed close in, the Kerry campaign was even more unwieldy and clumsy than it appeared in plain view. An underreported story of the campaign was the distracting presence of the candidate's willful wife, Teresa Heinz Kerry, who demanded everyone's attention, including her husband's. Kerry was delighted by Teresa, and not just by her fortune; she was smart, sexy and independent. But at times she could be a trial. Kerry himself was a loner, willing to be criticized but oddly impervious to criticism. The candidate was almost impossible to "manage," at least until the fall of 2004, when John Sasso arrived on the campaign plane to impose some discipline. It was a good thing Sasso came aboard with less than 60 days to go, observed Jim Jordan, Kerry's first campaign manager (fired after nine months in 2003); any longer and Kerry would have tired of him, too.

PRESIDENT BUSH, by contrast to Senator Kerry, was a zealot for order. The hard-drinking frat boy had long since found the cleansing joy of discipline. He demanded a tightly wound, top-down, on-time-to-the-minute operation. His advisers, some of them martinets, gave him what he wanted. At Bush-Cheney 2004 headquarters in Arlington, Va., the dress code was corporate and the atmosphere vaguely martial. Staffers were supposed to be upbeat at all times. The press was at best a nuisance to be tolerated. (Periodically, *Newsweek* would be banished from campaign headquarters, the last time because the magazine reported that a couple of campaign staffers had been seen twirling their cigars at a party before the first debate.)

Better organized than the Kerry campaign, more clever and quicker to respond, the Bush campaign became too confident, openly condescending toward the sometimes hapless Kerryites. It was almost too successful in creating, in the public mind, a caricature of Kerry as a loser. When, at the first debate, Kerry appeared more presidential than the president, the Bush campaign was stricken with near panic. It rallied by becoming even harsher in its treatment of Kerry. And Kerry slammed right back, as if to show he could mislead as shamelessly as his opponent. There were undoubtedly great issues of war and peace at stake in the election, but the attacks were highly personal, right up to the day the votes were cast.

Bush had the advantage of being a better natural campaigner than Kerry, who never did learn how to deliver a speech. Campaigning ground Kerry down; he seemed to labor under the weight of expectation. But Bush was worn by war and burdened by the terrible weight of the terrorist threat—and that was before he began stumping for re-election. Both men had deep reserves of grit and ambition. The ugly race did not necessarily reflect the character of the candidates. Both have a sense of honor, even if their better sides were sometimes hidden. In the end it was Kerry who had to find the moral fortitude to accept reality—and abandon a dream he had begun nurturing in high school.

Campaigning for the presidency is grueling beyond all imagining. It takes an extraordinary person to withstand the grind, the abuse or the pressure. Kerry and Bush, for all their human flaws and foibles, are not ordinary men. They are driven—by patriotism, duty, vanity, vision and, in this election, a lifelong disdain for each other. Each man saw in the other a world view he utterly rejected. Their personal differences, writ large, became the choice on Election Day, 2004.

Election
2004

Real deal: Staid and buttoned up, he hid a passionate, audacious side

ONE

The Democrats:
Fits and Starts

John Kerry thought the nomination was his
but didn't count on Howard Dean.
He made a hard charge for the finish line
as Dean's campaign imploded.

JOHN KERRY DIDN'T WANT to get on his own campaign
bus. It was just after Labor Day 2003, and the day before, Kerry had formally launched his candidacy with a
forgettable speech, delivered while standing in front of an
aircraft carrier in Charleston, S.C. Now, as he was preparing
to leave a rally in Manchester, N.H., Kerry strongly objected
to the slogan plastered on the side of the bus: COURAGE
EQUALS KERRY. He was traveling with his Vietnam buddies,
and combat veterans didn't like advertising themselves that
way, he protested. Real warriors—men who have actually
been shot at—don't care to brag, or even much talk about it.
Kerry was in a funk. He stood outside the bus, refusing to

get on while he complained about the posters advertising his personal courage. "You have to get on the bus," quietly insisted his top adviser, Bob Shrum. "I'll get on the staff bus," Kerry pouted.

His handlers had seen it before. Kerry did not like to play the brave war hero. His pollster, Mark Mellman, had tested a theme line—"John Kerry has the courage to do what's right for America"—and voters seemed to like it. But Kerry didn't. He was uncomfortable with showy displays of any kind, but especially ones that glorified his combat record. Jim Margolis, his paid media man, was eager to make ads using the almost three hours of film footage Kerry had shot with a handheld super-8 camera in Vietnam. The catch was that only about 15 seconds showed Kerry. "Goddammit, John, didn't you want to send anything home to your parents, for God's sake?" Margolis complained. Kerry answered, "No, that isn't what I was trying to do." He had wanted to capture his experiences—the countryside, the Vietnamese people, the ravages of war. Not to show off himself.

KERRY DIDN'T WANT TO TALK about the war. And yet he seemed to talk about it all the time, constantly reminding voters that he (unlike most other politicians, including George W. Bush) had fought for his country. Evoking his war record had been his trump card at critical moments in his political career. (In his hotly contested 1996 Senate re-election campaign, his opponent, popular Massachusetts Gov. Bill Weld, criticized Kerry's opposition to the death penalty.

Kerry gravely intoned, "I know something about killing . . .") Chris Heinz, Teresa Heinz Kerry's 31-year-old son, who enjoyed a teasing, macho relationship with his stepfather, bluntly warned Kerry that the press was beginning to view Kerry's frequent evocations of his Vietnam service as a tired cliché. To some of Kerry's aides, the senator seemed almost bipolar about his war record: on the one hand, the strong silent type; on the other, living proof that the Vietnam War will never end.

To show off—or not? To be proud—or humble? To strut—or self-deprecate? Sometimes Kerry seemed torn by conflicting impulses, and not just about his war record. Like every politician, he yearned to be noticed. The wise guys of the Massachusetts media and political establishment made fun of Kerry for hogging the limelight: they called him "Live Shot." As a legislator he was not a backroom dealmaker. He liked to be out front, conducting high-profile investigations of hot topics like allegations of drug running by the CIA. And yet he was capable of small acts of modesty and decency, of giving credit to others, and he often seemed uneasy before a camera or a microphone.

Kerry's ambivalence helps explain why he is not a natural politician. Kerry cannot sit still. He must always be up and doing, and he has been running for president, depending on whom you believe, since he was 14 years old, 18 at the latest. He was mocked for his ambition ("JFK," it was said, stood for "Just For Kerry"). Yet his more perceptive schoolmates always sensed that he was listening to some inner voice, telling him not to give in to the siren song of self-promotion.

It is the same stern, patrician voice—preaching modesty, humility, duty—that whispered into the ears of generations of privileged youth of the old WASP ascendancy, including generations of Bushes. "I do not want to hear the Great I Am," Dorothy Walker Bush, mother and grandmother of presidents, had scolded her son George if he bragged too much about his sporting triumphs as a schoolboy in the 1930s and 1940s.

Though Kerry liked to play down his elitist side—his accent, pure Thurston Howell III as a young man, became less plummy over time—he never shed all the trappings of his social class, or tried to. To his classmates Kerry had been a bit of an outsider, the fruit of some Brahmin seed (a Winthrop and a Forbes on his mother's side, but he learned only late in life that he was Jewish on his father's side), and he was never as well off as most of his classmates. They thought he tried a little too hard to show that he really belonged and, by striving, betrayed his insecurity. The WASP ascendancy was beginning its decline when Kerry graduated from the poshest of the New England prep schools, St. Paul's, in 1962, but its gentleman's code of muscular Christianity was still strong. Episcopal Church schools like St. Paul's tried to teach the virtue of humility, the sin of pride, the value of quiet service to others . . .

That is, up to a point. Ruling-class sons were supposed to compete hard—but not sweat too much. To get (or stay) ahead—but do so gracefully, even effortlessly. To wear the mantle of wealth and power lightly, coolly. The style had been set by an earlier generation of swells who had fashioned certain unwritten, strict yet ambiguous rules of decorum. It was all very complicated, a tricky, delicate business of flaunting it, but subtly, and John Forbes Kerry, at least in the critical eyes of his classmates, never seemed to get the balance right. While other preppies had been perfecting their slouches on the greenswards of country clubs, Kerry had been grimly learning a more Puritan code, like how to navigate a small boat in the fog off the New England coast, doggedly trying to please his dour and secretive father. His mother sweetly preached the duty to serve and the old-time virtue of choosing the harder right over the easier wrong. (Her last words to her son, says Kerry, were "Integrity, integrity, integrity.") Their son was a good boy at school, a striver and serious, delivering a speech on "The Plight of the Negro" and founding a debating society. But he was too earnest, too obvious for the cutups, who mocked the faint air of superiority that Kerry wore, mostly as a defense.

Kerry's revenge was to do better, to excel, to leave his detractors behind—but not to boast! Never to gloat! Unless, of course, boasting was absolutely necessary to get ahead. There was something a little desperate, but admirable, about Kerry's determination. He would do what it took to get where he wanted to go.

In New Hampshire that day after Labor Day 2003, he got on the bus.

Kerry had been assured that the nomination was his, almost, as it were, by right. A memo drafted by his campaign manager, Jim Jordan, in November 2002 assured him that he would be "the first one out of the box" in the upcoming campaign and that he would raise the most money "because you're the best candidate." He would establish himself as front runner, soak up endorsements and contributions and march inexorably to the nomination.

It was all myth. Former Vermont governor Howard Dean, blunt and down to earth (especially in comparison with the lordly Kerry), had burst from the pack with a grass-roots Internet-fueled campaign and huge outdoor rallies on his Sleepless Summer tour in August. The establishment press swooned over the anti-establishment candidate. Kerry was deemed a hopeless stiff, his campaign written off as moribund.

Kerry was nonplused by it all, a little hurt that Dean had run as the "movement" candidate against Kerry, the tool of the Washington status quo. Kerry had been in the Senate for 20 years, but he still saw himself as the reform-minded anti-war protester who had come from Vietnam, tossed away his ribbons and defied the Nixon administration. (Dean had fun with Kerry's self-righteousness; at his private debate prep, he would pose as Kerry, sticking his nose up in the air and mimicking Kerry: "I was in Vietnam; I don't take any PAC money.")

Kerry didn't know what to do about Dean. His own advisers were divided. Most of the pros, his paid political consultants and campaign manager, wanted to go negative. The philosophy of Chris Lehane, one of his media advisers, was "You either hit or you're being hit." The hawks wanted to go at Dean from the left, to convince voters that Dean was not a true liberal. "We didn't want to rip the guy's face off," said

Jordan, "but he wasn't going away, and we had to strip at least a third of his liberal support away."

On the other side, leading the so-called pacifists, was Bob Shrum, widely regarded as Kerry's most important adviser. (After the election, Kerry described Shrum as "one of my most important advisers. I don't have just one.") Shrum is the brand name among big-money Democratic campaign consultants, the most-sought-after hired gun, brilliant and fluent but also insecure. He was Kerry's friend, his peer; everyone else was Kerry's employee. Staffers crossed Shrum at their peril. Edgy and superstitious, Shrum prefers, in tense moments, to wear a fuchsia scarf given to him by Washington superlawyer Robert Bennett—even in the middle of summer. He had forgotten to take his lucky scarf to Nashville on election night 2000, and he wasn't going to make that mistake again. Shrum had worked on the successful political campaigns of a third of the U.S. Senate. But when it came to presidential politics, his luck had not been good. He was 0 for 7 (his past clients included Ed Muskie, Ted Kennedy, Bob Kerrey, Dick Gephardt and Al Gore).

SHRUM WAS A GIFTED WORDSMITH, the inheritor of the Sorensonian mantle, crafter of lofty phrases and speeches filled with the lift of a driving dream (which, after a time, started to sound alike, no matter whose lips uttered them). He had written Ted Kennedy's famous "Sail against the wind" speech in 1980, and politicians had lined up ever since, hoping that Shrum could make them eloquent, too. Shrum wanted to ignore Dean and take the high road with a series of "Great Speeches" about the future of the country. It was somewhat uncharacteristic for Shrum to argue against slashing attacks; he was known for taking a "people against the powerful" populist line. But his intuition told him that by demolishing Dean, the Kerry camp would only open the way for a late surge by Sen. John Edwards of North Carolina, a young but honey-tongued populist with a seemingly boundless future. (In the so-called Shrum primary, Kerry and Edwards had vied for the services of the superconsultant; Shrum had initially leaned toward Edwards.) When Team Kerry met in the summer and fall of 2003, Shrum acidly undercut the hawks who wanted to trash and burn Dean. "What do you want to do?" he asked. "Elect Edwards?"

For months, as Kerry sank in the polls and Dean soared, the argument rattled on inside the Kerry camp. Campaign manager Jordan was an old political hand who had served as staff director of the Democratic Senate Campaign Committee. A soft-spoken but hard-nosed operative from North Carolina, Jordan admired Kerry, but he was weary of his indecisiveness. "The world around Kerry is a lot of white males talking," he groused. Every time Jordan decided something, the person who lost out went behind his back to appeal to Kerry, who spent inordinate amounts of time on his cell phone not resolving various disputes. Kerry was known for being deliberative—he was proud of it—but Jordan despaired that Kerry had been turned into a caricature of the U.S. Senate. Kerry's didactic, overlong speeches, his insistence on explaining every nuance of his rational thought process (while not revealing much of his true feelings), reinforced his image as a windbag. Jordan was blunt with Kerry, telling him that voters in focus groups said "they don't understand you, you won't shut up, you sound like a politician."

For the Labor Day announcement speech, the hawks presented a draft meant to be sharp and punchy, with lines like "Spring training is over" and "My mother was an environmental activist before it was cool." Shrum dismissed the speech as "sophomoric." At midnight before the speech, Shrum arrived at Kerry's house in Boston—he had taken a two-hour cab ride from Cape Cod—to insist that *his* speech be used, untouched. Jordan objected; Shrum's speech was "flowery bulls—t," he said. A compromise draft was cobbled together. The reception was at best ho-hum.

Kerry was fading fast. The press got wind of the infighting and began retelling a joke (planted by the Dean campaign) that Kerry's campaign was like Noah's Ark—two of everything—as Kerry straddled the advice given him and tried to please everyone. "I couldn't get the man to make decisions," said Jordan.

By NOVEMBER, however, Kerry was finally getting ready to make one decision: to fire Jordan. As early as July, Kerry had approached his political mentor, Ted Kennedy, and asked his advice about replacing Jordan. Kennedy told him he thought a change was long overdue. Kennedy was an avuncular figure to Kerry. In an interview with *Newsweek* in June 2004, Kerry went on and on about how he had studied Kennedy, a legendary storyteller and schmoozer, trying to learn from the senior senator from Massachusetts (40 years in office) that in the end it was "the people" that mattered, not so much one's policy views. But Kerry was uncomfortable with personal confrontation. He kept giving Jordan more rope. In the end, Jordan hanged himself.

The campaign manager's first mistake was to underestimate the Internet revolution of the Deaniacs. "There are no votes on the Internet," Jordan had said back in the spring of 2003. At a meeting of top staffers and advisers at Kerry's house on Nantucket over the Fourth of July, Kerry asked for a show of hands. How many thought Dean had crossed over from fringe candidate to serious contender? Kerry raised his own hand high. The candidate may not have been a natural politician, but he was able to spot the power of the Internet, particularly as a fund-raising tool, before most of his advisers did.

Jordan's second fatal error was more personal. He alienated the candidate's family. Kerry is something of a loner; unlike most presidential candidates, he does not have a longtime political *consigliere* or friend who regularly travels with him on the plane. His only consistent adviser was his brother, Cameron, a Boston lawyer, a low-key figure who was devoted but not politically savvy. Jordan did not have much use for Cam. "He's no Robert Kennedy," said Jordan, and to Kerry, bluntly: "Keep your brother out of my way."

Kerry bridled at Jordan's impertinence, and he was especially protective of his wife, Teresa, who often clashed with Jordan. Teresa could be an earth mother, warm and funny, sometimes in an oddball way, and embracing to her friends and family. She liked to hand out her recipe for "Mama T's brownies" (she has 26 godchildren, who call her Mama T). But, in the manner of the very rich, she had an air of entitlement, a sharp temper, and she was known for keeping people, including her husband, waiting. The staff regarded her as something of a hypochondriac, and she canceled three trips in October—to Arizona, Pennsylvania and New Mexico—at the last minute, usually for what was described to aides as a "nonspecific malady."

Kerry seemed to be walking on eggshells around Teresa. He wanted her to be happy, in part because she was much more trouble on the campaign trail when she was unhappy. Teresa had a way of letting everyone know that Kerry was her second husband, and that she still loved her first, Sen. John Heinz, who died in a plane crash in 1991. Teresa above all valued her own candor. She wanted to be able to talk about her Botox injections and yak with women reporters about her views on reincarnation and the pros and cons of hormone-replacement therapy. She did not want to hear about "message discipline." Indeed, her frankness could be refreshing. Some crowds responded with "you go, girl" enthusiasm when she made fun of her husband and voiced a strong opinion on the trail. But others wondered why the slightly eccentric woman introducing the candidate was prattling on about herself in a difficult-to-understand accent. She was not one for the plastic, adoring smile of the traditional candidate's wife. On the other hand, Kerry's handlers wondered, did she have to look sullen?

At one point in the summer, as Dean was starting to pull away, Teresa called Jordan and demanded, "I want you to issue a challenge for me to debate Howard Dean." (John Kerry later said that his wife had been "just joking.") Jordan was less than diplomatic in telling her it was a crazy idea, and he had a little too much fun sharing the moment with other campaign officials. Jordan's e-mails trashing the candidate's wife, or word of them, inevitably reached his rivals—including Bob Shrum. An old friend of Teresa's from the Georgetown chattering-class party circuit, Shrum understood her moods and saw her importance to Kerry. Teresa and Shrum enjoyed drinking vintage wine together and commiserating about Jordan, sealing his fate.

Late-night comics liked to joke that Kerry had married Teresa for her money to pay for his presidential race. (Jay Leno: "[Kerry] once raised $500 million with two words: 'I do.'") But, in fact, Kerry had signed a prenuptial agreement that kept almost all of Teresa's fortune (inherited from her first husband, the Heinz ketchup heir) in her hands. Under the campaign-finance laws, Teresa could give the Kerry campaign no more than any other donor—$2,000. True, the system is full of loopholes. Teresa could have found a legal dodge to use her vast fortune to help Kerry—she could have established some kind of trust in his name—and, indeed, she had vowed to spend her money if Kerry's opponents tried to destroy his character. But the "optics" of such a move, as the media consultants liked to say, would be terrible. It would vindicate all those late-night jokes about Kerry as a kept man.

KERRY WOULD HAVE TO FIND some other way to raise the money to pay for his campaign. He was not a rich man when he married Teresa. He was confined by the campaign-finance laws, which matched what a candidate could raise by private sources up to $18.7 million, but put a cap on spending in each primary state ($729,000 for New Hampshire, $1.3 million for Iowa).

Kerry had been a strong supporter of campaign-finance reform, but like any presidential hopeful, he envied George W. Bush—who, as a candidate in 2000, had raised so much money he didn't need matching funds from the Feds. A candidate could opt out of the campaign-finance system—"bust the caps," in campaign jargon. With his Internet money machine, Howard Dean was on track to raise more than $50 million before the first primary, and in November he decided to abandon the federal campaign-finance system so he could spend it all. On Nov. 6 and 7 he held a laughable Internet "plebiscite" to get permission from his faithful Deaniacs (most of whom were pro campaign-finance reform but were willing to put aside their scruples to win).

Jordan had been trying to conserve Kerry's money so that there would be enough left to buy ads after the primaries began. Shrum was agitating to spend more money on TV advertising, and he wanted to bust the caps. Shrum's partner, Tad Devine, put it to Kerry. Devine, a seasoned political hand who had effectively run the Gore campaign in 2000, was known for being willing to speak truth to power. In late October, Devine told Kerry: get out of the campaign-finance limits or get out of the race. (After the election, Kerry insisted to *Newsweek* that he had always intended to opt out of the campaign finance system, as long as Dean went first.)

Kerry seemed to be "hand-wringing and dithering," said Jordan. "John's not an instinctive politician. He doesn't understand the rhythms of a campaign. He's a very gifted man in ways that are more analogous to being a good president than a good campaigner."

In fact, Kerry was following a familiar path on the campaign trail. A lackluster beginning—and, just as it seemed to be almost too late, a hard charge for the finish line. On Saturday, Nov. 8, he summoned Jordan to Boston and fired him. Kerry started by flattering Jordan, but then he insisted that Jordan resign and tell people it was his idea. Jordan refused, and the frustrations bubbled up. ("We did plenty of screaming at each other, and toward the end the 'f— yous' got kind of loud," said Jordan.) Two weeks later, Kerry opted out of federal financing and began the arduous business of trying to raise tens of millions of dollars and to resuscitate a campaign that was widely regarded as doomed.

First came some discipline. Ted Kennedy's no-nonsense chief of staff, Mary Beth Cahill, took over as campaign manager. (She had been watching the campaign, she said, with a "horrified fascination.") Cahill, white-haired and matronly in a steely sort of way, shut off the back channels to Kerry by turning off his cell phone and letting it be known, like a nun rapping knuckles, that she would not tolerate any more petty bickering.

Then came a marked improvement in the candidate. Kerry's speechwriter, Andrei Cherny, had been trying to think of a way to convey that Kerry was ready to go toe to toe with President Bush on national security, the Democrats' weakest front. The expression "Bring it on" popped into his head. He wrote the line into a Kerry speech to be delivered to the Democratic National Committee in October, but Shrum crossed it out. "Bush-type bravado," he sneered—too undignified for Kerry.

But with the press reporting his campaign in melt-down, Kerry needed to do something to change his lackluster style, and at the Jefferson-Jackson Day dinner in Des Moines on Nov. 15, he used Cherny's "Bring it on" line. The crowd loved it. (Kerry later apologized to Cherny for not using the line earlier. "I was wrong," he said. A few months later, Cherny was shuffled off to work at the DNC.)

Strong, crisp—and presidential—Kerry was a hit at the JJ dinner, an important annual rite and showplace for the candidates. Kerry's campaign packed the crowd with supporters chanting "Real deal," Kerry's latest slogan (the real deal: that is, a candidate who could win the following November, unlike Dean). It was a sign, if anyone had been looking, that Kerry should not be counted out. There were other omens that the race was far from over. Before the dinner, a curious event took place. The Dean campaign, eager to show off its vast army of Deaniacs, took reporters out on the skywalk in downtown Des Moines to watch 40-plus yellow school buses rumble into town—shock troops in the Dean onslaught to get out the vote for the January Iowa caucuses, the first electoral test on the road to the nomination. One of the reporters noticed something odd. "Is it just me, or are they empty?" asked Liz Marlantes of *The Christian Science Monitor.* The other reporters tried to peer through the tinted-glass windows. All they could see was row after row of empty seats.

But in New Hampshire, Dean's polls continued to soar, while Kerry's remained flat. The press had already begun to look for someone else to play the role of spoiler to Dean, maybe Gen. Wesley Clark, who had entered the race late (in September), stumbled about as a campaign neophyte, but still held allure for Democrats paranoid about their own perceived weakness on national security. The capture of Iraqi strongman Saddam Hussein on Dec. 13 made Democrats despondent. Iraq was looking like a worthy cause after all; the violence seemed to be abating there. Bush looked invincible. Actually, Saddam's capture was good news for Kerry: it helped remind Democrats that in the end the nominee had to be electable, and that Dean was too far to the left and Clark was unready for the national political stage.

All this would become clear—in perfect hindsight. On Dec. 9 Al Gore showed the political fingertips that lost him the 2000 election. He endorsed Howard Dean, probably at the precise moment when Dean had peaked and was about to head down. Gore's endorsement came as a blow to Kerry, who had thought Gore was his friend, or at least his political ally. When the Kerry camp heard the rumors that Gore was endorsing Kerry's opponent, Kerry tried to call the former veep to find out if it could be true. Kerry had Gore's cellphone number and called him. "This is John Kerry," he said when Gore answered. The phone went dead. Kerry tried to call several more times and never got through. He was hurt. "I endorsed him early. I was up for consideration as his running mate," he complained to an aide.

Kerry's revival was underway, slowly—imperceptibly to the press and the political establishment. Back in September he had made the brave—and difficult—decision to bet most of his resources on Iowa, not New Hampshire. Kerry had been expected to do well in his neighboring state, but he was getting drubbed by Vermonter Dean. (One poll showed Dean at 45 percent in the Granite State, Kerry at 10 percent; nationally, Kerry was about even with Al Sharpton.) He needed to do something to change the dynamic. He needed to win somewhere else.

Polling for the Iowa caucuses is notoriously difficult: it is hard to measure whether people will actually show up in the middle of January to spend two or three hours to cast their votes. But Kerry's pollster, Mark Mellman, had begun to notice that on a comparative basis, Kerry was doing better versus Dean in Iowa than in New Hampshire. The only way to come back in New Hampshire, he reasoned, was to create a slingshot effect, to pick up enough momentum in the Iowa caucuses to convince New Hampshire voters, who went to the polls a week later, that Kerry was the only electable candidate. "Iowa is the key to New Hampshire," Mellman told the Kerry team.

That meant shifting the campaign's limited resources to Iowa—in effect, to bet it all on the quirky Iowa caucuses. There was really no choice, argued Mellman. "There are two things we could do in New Hampshire," he argued at a strategy meeting in September. "One, we could save a drowning child in the Merrimack River [which runs through southern New Hampshire]. Second, we could have him [Kerry] do well in Iowa. The second is easier to arrange."

Kerry was persuaded, but barely, and by December he was having second thoughts. Losing New Hampshire would be a painful humiliation for him. "We need to be in New Hampshire," he would say. He was gambling more than his name. He had taken a $6 million mortgage on the house in Boston to bring some desperately needed cash into the campaign. (Under the prenup, Kerry had part ownership in one of Teresa's five houses.) His brother, Cam, worried that Kerry was betting his daughters' inheritance in a game he could not win. In early January, Kerry's best friend from school days and his former brother-in-law, David Thorne, spoke with Shrum about whether Kerry really had a chance of winning. "I'm worried about the situation in Iowa," said Shrum, "If the numbers don't start to improve, I really feel you should tell your friend John that he shouldn't spend his money."

Shrum knew it wasn't hopeless yet, though, in part because he knew Kerry. He understood that at just such moments Kerry had a way of rallying, of rising to the challenge, of even enjoying the sensation of risk and trying to control the uncontrollable. The staid, buttoned-up Kerry concealed a more passionate, audacious side. Shrum, a romantic, had been drawn to the Kennedys as a young theology student/ law graduate turned politico. Kerry was not JFK—Kerry's own idol as a teen—but the similarities were more than superficial. Both JFKs liked fine and stylish people and things, thought deeply about history and the world—and were not afraid of risk.

Kerry does not like the daredevil label. He emphatically rejected it in an interview with *Newsweek*, saying that he avoided really dangerous sports (he mentioned bungee jumping) and was always in control when he took on scary-seeming physical challenges, like kite boarding (a kind of airborne windsurfing). But control is a relative thing, and Kerry clearly likes to look for the edge. For instance, he said he performed aerial stunts only in a plane above 5,000 feet, so that if something went wrong, he'd have time to parachute.

BEFORE CHRISTMAS, Shrum drove back to Boston from New Hampshire with John and Teresa and stayed at the house on Louisburg Square, the one Kerry had mortgaged, an elegant brick mansion in the old Brahmin quarter of Beacon Hill. It was snowy outside, and the old friends opened a bottle of wine and began reminiscing. They recalled an earlier crisis, in the fall of 1996, when Kerry had been faltering in his Senate re-election race against Governor Weld. Kerry had invited Shrum to dinner and asked him to take over the campaign. He had shoved a poll across the table and said,

"We're behind in 14 of the 15 internals"—the important polling benchmarks on questions like "Who do you trust more?" and "Who is a better leader?"

With Shrum's help, Kerry had rallied in the 1996 Senate race, as he always had, and beaten Weld cleanly. "I've been in tougher situations than this before," Kerry said that snowy evening, as he, Teresa and Shrum sat around sipping their good wine in front of the fire. Shrum knew that Kerry was thinking about Vietnam. "When he's in a tough situation, he thinks at least they're not shooting bullets," says Shrum.

Shrum had taken some more tangible comfort from his friend the pollster Stan Greenberg, who believed that the voters of Iowa would inevitably take a second look and ask: Who is presidential? Who can take on Bush? Kerry needed to be there, front and center, because the answer would not be Howard Dean.

Few people knew it at the time, but the Dean campaign was imploding. The Deaniac movement had been in large part a creation of political grass-roots mastermind Joe Trippi. A creative genius, Trippi did not sleep and appeared to live on Diet Pepsi, consuming at least a dozen a day. Pepsi cans were strewn around his office and arrayed along his desk, where the empties were used as receptacles for wads of Skoal chewing tobacco. ("This campaign is all about getting me a gig as a Pepsi spokesman," he quipped to a reporter.) He had once fallen asleep while standing and hit the floor with such force that he cracked a rib. Trippi's caffeinated rages, fueled by his off-the-charts blood sugar (a diabetic, he was dangerously careless about taking his medications), reduced his assistant to tears. Once, after he overturned his desk, she fled out the door and did not return for three days.

Dean was in some ways the accidental candidate. Truth be told, he wasn't really the red-hot revolutionary of the Deaniacs' fevered hopes. He was a moderate, fiscally conservative small-state governor who had been swept up in a wave not entirely of his own making. He and Trippi never worked well together. Dean was a micro-manager who refused to give Trippi control of the campaign checkbook. Management was not Trippi's strong suit; the campaign, badly run, burned through its $40 million war chest. By October, Dean and Trippi were speaking to each other only when they had to, and Trippi was threatening to quit.

The closer Dean came to actually winning the nomination, the more he seemed to misstep, to blurt out something that the gaffe hunters in the press could hang around his neck. Dean had always been a loose cannon. In the summer of 2002, his aides had been relieved that no cameras had captured the would-be Democratic nominee, in full cry at a gay fund-raiser on New York's Fire Island, shouting out, "If Bill Clinton could be the first black president, I can be the first gay president!" But now the press was circling, and he seemed to recoil. In December, Trippi told his aides, Dean had come to him and tearfully confessed that he had run only to shake up the Democratic Party and push for health-care reform, that he never cared about being president and never thought he could win. ("That's a figment of Joe's imagination," Dean told *Newsweek*. "I mean, Joe just made that up out of whole cloth.")

By then Trippi's loyalty really lay less with Dean than with the cybermovement he had built. Dean was irritated by Trippi's celebrity (the campaign manager was often wired for a CNN documentary and had to be reminded to turn off the mike when he went to the bathroom). By early January, Trippi was in a deep gloom, and so were his closest campaign associates. One senior aide compared the Dean campaign to the novel *Flowers for Algernon,* the story of a seriously retarded man who, put through a course of radically experimental treatment, lives for a few months as a genius—then regresses rapidly to what he had been before the experts remade him: a moron.

Trippi was planning on retiring to his farm in Maryland after the New Hampshire primary. Still, he wanted to take one last shot, to "bet it all" on Iowa and New Hampshire, knowing that in a protracted fight Dean's candor would kill him. "It's probably a f—ing miracle we're even sitting where we're at," he said, utterly despondent. He fell silent for a while. "The guy," Trippi said suddenly, referring to Dean, "is not ready for prime time. I mean, he's just f—ing not ready for prime time, and he never will be." There were 11 days left before the Iowa caucuses.

D EAN'S PLAN IN IOWA was to flood the state with an army of volunteers, in jaunty orange caps, to knock on doors and personally escort voters to the polls. Kerry's Iowa organizer, Michael Whouley, was appropriately skeptical of the Dean approach in small rural towns where out-of-state college kids were regarded as aliens. A legendary political figure who avoided most reporters (thus enhancing the legend), Whouley was patient and quiet, but he had an aura of confidence. On the Friday night before Christmas he gathered 80 field staffers in a Unitarian church in downtown Des Moines and told them, "It's never a guy with the early momentum. It's the guy with the late momentum, and that's us."

As he crisscrossed Iowa, Kerry was a much more engaged and relaxed campaigner. He seemed bemused and affectionate with Teresa, not quite so nervous about her mood. "C'mon, General, let's go," he said, patting her on the back and marching her onstage at a campaign event in Iowa in early January. He told the women in the room that he wouldn't see his wife again until after the caucuses; the ladies made an "awww" sound. Teresa smirked and made a "no big deal" gesture.

The traveling press continued to have doubts about Teresa. After one particularly disjointed speech at the Hotel Fort Des Moines in early January, press aide David Wade paced nervously while reporters snickered that the candidate's wife was on medication. But the press was warming to Kerry. He had begun traveling with an old friend from his antiwar days, Peter Yarrow of the folk group Peter, Paul and Mary. Kerry had played bass in his prep-school rock-and-roll band, and to relax he liked to strum a guitar and sing along with Yarrow. The old folkie seemed to make Kerry nostalgic and remember his roots as an authentic movement figure. (When Yarrow played "Puff the Magic Dragon," a CBS camera caught Kerry playfully miming that he was toking on a joint.) On one frozen night, heading down desolate Route 63, an exhausted Kerry and his staff and the traveling press passed out cold Budweisers and chocolate cake. "Pedro," Kerry said, "get your guitar." Late into the songs, Yarrow played "Carry on My Sweet Survivor":

> Carry on my sweet survivor
> Carry on my lonely friend
> Don't give up the dream and
> Don't you let it end

"Was the struggle worth the cost?" Yarrow asked Kerry. "Yes, Peter, it was," said Kerry softly. Even the most jaded reporters sat quietly for a moment.

Despite Kerry's uneasiness over playing up his war exploits, the campaign had been airing an ad showing one of his old Swift Boat crewmen, Dale Sandusky, saying that Kerry's boldness and decisiveness had "saved our lives" in Vietnam. Here was the way to get around Kerry's reticence: have his crewmates speak for him. The ad was a success. Iowa voters who had seen the ad favored Kerry by almost 20 points.

The best testimonial came by pure luck. In Oregon in early January, a retired policeman named Jim Rassmann was in a bookstore and noticed a book about Kerry's Vietnam experience by historian Douglas Brinkley, *Tour of Duty*. Rassmann had been a Special Forces soldier who had fallen off Kerry's boat during a fire fight in the delta. Kerry had swung his boat around and come back to rescue Rassmann. His arm injured, Kerry himself had pulled Rassmann out of the water. Rassmann thumbed through the index of *Tour of Duty* and saw his story. On a whim, he called the Kerry campaign and said he'd like to help. The receptionist, Jackie Williams, had the presence to get hold of the campaign's veterans coordinator. Rassmann was in Iowa the next day, flown there by the campaign. (Briefing Rassmann, a Kerry aide asked if he'd ever been in front of cameras. "Yes, usually after somebody's been killed," the ex-cop drolly replied. He had worked as a homicide investigator.)

Kerry was genuinely surprised to encounter Rassmann, whom he had not seen since 1969. Their reunion, a warm hug, was on television all over the state. The caucuses were only two days away.

On caucus night, as they were riding in a darkened bus in Des Moines, a Fox News producer handed Shrum the entrance polls. Kerry 29, Edwards 21, Dean 20, Gephardt 15. Shrum later recalled that he felt like crying. He showed the numbers to Kerry, who extended a wordless high-five.

T HE RACE WAS, for all practical purposes, over. The Dean scream, uttered a few hours later as Dean tried to rally his crestfallen troops, was mostly theater; the damage had been done. Dean had finished with 18 percent of the vote at the Iowa caucuses. The press, and most Democrats, wrote him off. Edwards would make a good showing in the primaries ahead, but he didn't have the money or the presidential gravitas to overtake Kerry.

Kerry was in the shower the next week when he won in New Hampshire, the state that had seemed so hopeless only a month before. With the campaign short of funds, he had been staying at the Tage Inn in Manchester, a bare-bones establishment, and on some mornings the showers had run cold. On primary night the hot water was working, and Kerry was enjoying it, leaving the bathroom door ajar so he could hear the television. Shrum and Teresa were in the room watching when ABC called New Hampshire for Kerry. There was a shriek from the shower. "Oh, God, I've won the New Hampshire primary!" he yelled. For once, Kerry let himself gloat.

TWO

The President: Inner Circle

*Bush's team was upbeat. But not everyone
was sure about the race.*

ARL ROVE CALLED THE GROUP "the Breakfast
Club." They met at Rove's unadorned house in
northwest Washington on Saturday, Dec. 13, 2003,
the day Saddam Hussein was captured in Iraq. It had already
been a week of cheering news for the Bush-Cheney 2004
campaign. A few days earlier, former vice president Al Gore
had endorsed the Democratic front runner, Howard Dean.
The Democratic establishment seemed to be lining up behind Dean. The Bush-Cheney campaign could only pray
that the Democrats would not come to their senses. Rove's
team had already assembled a phone-book-thick volume of
opposition research on Dean, titled "Howard Dean Un-
sealed: Second Edition, Wrong for America" (on the cover
was a collage of 13 pictures of Dean looking addled). The

Bushies had been poring over footage of the former Vermont governor on the campaign trail. Adman Mark McKinnon's media team had cut a spot called "When Angry Democrats Attack!" featuring a wild Dean ranting and raving, and posted it on the Bush-Cheney Web site.

Rove had called this meeting of his top advisers to discuss all the ways they were going to bury Howard Dean. Matthew Dowd, the campaign's pollster and strategist, was known as a pessimist, but even he conceded to the group, "You have to give the direction arrow to Dean at this point."

The strategy was obvious: a barrage of ads featuring President Bush as "steady" and Dean as "reckless." The group laughed about some of the scripts they had cranked out for a campaign McKinnon was calling "Dean Unplugged." An early favorite, submitted by Fred Davis, a California adman known by the nickname Hollywood (he drove a Porsche, wore tinted sunglasses and had shared a suite in college with Paul Reubens, the actor better known as Pee-wee Herman), opened with the image of a mother anxiously flipping channels as her baby lies in a crib behind her. Howard Dean is on the TV screen, hyperventilating. The baby begins to fret and cry . . . then the voice of George W. Bush, strong, comforting, resolute, replaces Dean on the screen. The baby quiets and sleeps peacefully.

It was an open secret that Karl Rove was itching to take on Dean. Back in July, Rove had been seen standing in a crowd near his home in Washington, watching Dean pass by in an Independence Day parade. Rove was quoted as chortling: "Heh, heh, heh, that's the one we want. Go, Howard Dean!"

On message: Greeting troops in Colorado in the fall of 2003

Misquoted, Rove insisted to *Newsweek* (the witness, he claimed, was a "lefty," a Sierra Club member). Rove said he simply joined in the chanting, "Two, four, six, eight, why don't we all bloviate!"

"Bloviate" is a favorite Rove-ism. Others, often expressed by e-mail: "Yeah baby!" "Attawaytogo!" and, more obscurely, "It's Miller time!" Rove was the unquestioned boss of the campaign to re-elect the president. Everyone reported to him; even local GOP bosses checked with him before making a move. The group he gathered around his dining-room table this December morning was the tight little inner circle—Dowd, campaign manager Ken Mehlman, White House Communications Director Dan Bartlett, campaign communications director Nicolle Devenish. The group was secret at first; other top staffers only gradually learned of its existence. As winter turned to spring, Rove would occasionally add other guests. For a Republican, there was no greater call to duty than an invitation from Rove to join the Breakfast Club.

King Karl, ruler of a vast domain, was held in awe by all (except Bush, who from time to time referred to his chief political adviser as Turd Blossom). Rove had never stopped campaigning since the 2000 squeaker. From the moment he walked into the White House in 2001, he had been building the Republican base, the vast Red State army of evangelicals; flag-waving small-town and rural American Dreamers; '60s-hating, pro-death-penalty, anti-gay-marriage social conservatives; Big Donors—the new Republican majority, or so Rove hoped. A steady wave of e-mails (appropriately studded with

Rove-isms), notes, photos, anniversary cards and White House Christmas-party invitations stroked the faithful. But discipline was the key: Rove set up a reporting system designed to hold accountable party bosses and volunteers alike. He created the mystique of an all-seeing, all-knowing boss of bosses; if the emperor had no clothes, no one particularly wanted to find out.

A ROVE COLLEAGUE CALLED HIM "five-dimensional." His friends as well as his enemies described him as generous, crude, charming, repellent, thoughtful, vindictive, funny, mean, brilliant and foolish. Plump and balding, a jolly joker, he could be savage. In *Esquire* magazine, writer Ron Suskind recalled sitting outside Rove's office waiting for an interview to begin. Inside, he wrote, he could hear Rove bellowing at an aide, "We will f— him. Do you hear me? We will f— him. We will ruin him. Like no one has ever f—ed him!" (A White House spokesman has said that Suskind has a "hyperactive imagination.") But Rove was well aware of his reputation and cultivated it. On Halloween 2003, a *Newsweek* reporter teased Rove for not wearing a costume. "I'm scary enough," he replied.

Rove made little attempt to hide his feelings. Poking his head into the crowded press cabin on Air Force One during a trip on a frigid day in January, he snarled, "Weenies!" In December 2003 Rove's joy at the prospect of systematically destroying Dean was plain for all to see. After the capture of Saddam Hussein, the president's approval rating rose to 63 percent. As Dean continued to fulminate, as reporters no longer described his bluntness as "refreshing" and instead began the old gotcha game, jumping on the green governor's "gaffes," Rove & Co. watched as Dean's negative rating climbed to 39 percent.

Other advisers worried about too much of a good thing. Too much Republican gloating over a Dean candidacy might make the Democrats wake up. "We don't want to tip this thing too far," McKinnon, the campaign's chief media man, fretted in December. "Our concern is that it will collapse on him." But Rove didn't seem concerned. John Kerry had been the presumptive front runner back in the spring of 2003, but by autumn he was not even a blip on the radar screen. At strategy sessions of the Bush-Cheney campaign he was a "nonentity," recalled one Bush adviser. In October, Rove had said that Kerry had "p—ed away every advantage of the front runner." Wes Clark? "Imploded," Rove concluded. Joe Lieberman and John Edwards? "Nowhereville!" he exulted. (Most of the BC04 staff figured Edwards would be the toughest foe, but the North Carolina senator couldn't seem to raise money or get noticed.) Only Dick Gephardt, Rove thought, still had a chance, and not much of one. Rove was so convinced that Dean would be the president's foe in the general election that he began making small wagers around the White House, betting hamburgers that Dean would prevail.

As the holidays approached, the Bush White House was as jolly as Rove. On Dec. 20 the Bush daughters, Jenna and Barbara, both college seniors, decided to hold a blowout for their friends in the Executive Mansion. Jenna, a young lady with her father's eye for a good time, had heard about a band from Nashville that was a big favorite at Southern good-ole-boy fraternity parties. The band, formally called the Tyrone Smith Revue, was better known as Super T. The bandleader, Tyrone Smith, would appear for the second set wearing a red cape and a bright blue jumpsuit emblazoned with a giant T.

The Tyrone Smith Revue set up in the East Room, usually used for press conferences. Shortly after 9, when the drinks were flowing and the kids were starting to glow, Super T swung into "Shotgun" and summoned the president, the First Lady and the twins onto the stage. "I want the Secret Service to stay back!" he cried. "I'm taking over now!" Super T began to instruct the First Family in a dance called the Super T Booty Green. ("Put your hands on your knees. Bend over. Shake two times to the right, shake two times to the left.")

The First Family got right down. The crowd erupted. Super T picked up the beat; he later recalled hearing a familiar voice cry, "Go, Super T!" He looked back to see the president of the United States hollering and shaking it like in old times at the Deke House. Laura Bush gently put her hand on the president's elbow; the frat brother subsided; the chief executive returned to duty.

The Bushes went to bed that night at 11:30, about two hours after the president's usual bedtime. As he dozed off, or tried to, a conga line twisted along the red carpet he usually walked down for formal press conferences. (Before the president retired, Super T offered to play at the Inaugural. Bush just grinned.)

President Bush badly needed a break. Since 9/11 he had been obsessed. He began every morning by getting briefed on the so-called Threat Matrix, the CIA analysis of the threat of another terrorist attack. He saw himself as a war president in a war without end. "Terrorists declared war on the United States of America," Bush told audiences over and over during the fall of 2003. "And war is what they got!"

SOME OF HIS FRIENDS thought they saw less of his puckish humor, more of his impatience. The harder the choices, the worse the news, the more chaotic the world, the more stubbornly Bush demanded order in his own life. The onetime hard-drinking party boy was almost ascetic in his discipline: about getting exercise, about getting enough sleep, about having meetings start on time. He nicknamed his own chief of staff, Andy Card, "Tangent Man," for wandering off the subject. It was teasing with a hard edge. "He pays very close attention to his schedule, and if I'm not doing my job of monitoring his schedule, he disciplines me," said Card. All meetings started on time at the White House, or early. There all employees understood the Bush code: "Late is rude."

At the morning meeting with his staff, the talk increasingly turned to politics as the election year neared. Depending on what he had heard earlier at his threat briefing, Bush could be moody. "You can tell by his tone if he wants the long version or if he wants the short version," said an aide.

Sometimes Bush was blunt: "Y'all think this is worth wasting the president's time over?" he would ask when some minor matter came up. Rove was slowest to get the message. For all his political fingertips, Rove was obtuse in his inability, or unwillingness, to read the facial expressions of others. He would sometimes vex Bush by going on too long at meetings. "Karl sometimes doesn't get the signal," said the aide. Or maybe he was just obstinate.

Rove was constantly pushing the president to do more fund-raising. When it came to campaign finance, Rove believed in the Colin Powell Doctrine of Overwhelming Force—i.e., bury the enemy. In 2000 Bush had become the pre-emptive nominee by raising an astonishing war chest of more than $60 million before the campaign began. This time Rove wanted to have at least $150 million on hand to unleash a crushing ad blitz against the Democratic nominee, the minute one emerged.

The president, a homebody, loathed the fund-raising trips. "Another trip?" he would gripe as an aside to Card. Well, how about Laura? Rove would ask. "You will have to talk to the First Lady," Bush would teasingly grumble. "I'm not gonna mention that to her."

But in fact Laura Bush was, in her perfect-wife way, a good soldier. Again and again that fall and the following spring, the First Lady of the United States (FLOTUS, in White House speak) set off on Executive One Foxtrot, traveling under the Secret Service code name Tempo, with a hairstylist and a clutch of guards toting P90 submachine guns. On one trip, FLOTUS's press secretary, Gordon Johndroe, carried a small black case that looked like the bag the president used to carry the nuclear codes. "It's our football," joked Johndroe. The case contained the First Lady's makeup.

President Bush did not like to memorize lines. Mrs. Bush would smilingly rehearse them and speak them that night, word for word, as she posed with fat cats around the country. "We have a special treat for you tonight," her hosts would announce. The First Lady would come into the audience and stop at every table for a photo. It was a routine, repeated in country clubs and upscale hotel ballrooms coast to coast. Laura was unflagging. "She's tougher than the president," said one friend. "I've never seen her cry." She rarely complained, and took solace in small pleasures. After one particularly grueling day of meeting and greeting, she arrived at the Brentwood, Calif., home of a top GOP fundraiser, Brad Freeman. Concerned that the claws of their cat, Ernie, might scratch up the White House furniture, the Bushes had given their aging six-toed tabby to Freeman to take care of. Spotting Ernie, Laura swept the old fat cat into her arms. "Oh, Ernie!" she cried. "Do you remember me?" She looked over at Mercer Reynolds, the chief fund-raiser for the Bush-Cheney campaign. "Oh, he remembers me!" she exclaimed, a bit wistfully, to Reynolds. ("I'm not sure Ernie really remembers much of anything," said the moneyman, as he later recalled the scene.)

LAURA HAD ALWAYS BEEN PROTECTIVE of the twins. But they were 22 years old now, about to graduate from the

University of Texas and Yale, and attractive young women couldn't help but humanize the campaign. On the other hand, getting the girls involved could prove to be a disaster. In early winter, Gordon Johndroe went to Mrs. Bush with an interview request from a fashion magazine. He expected her to say no, as she always did, but instead she just said, "Why don't you call and ask the girls first?" The campaign had some reason to be anxious about the twins. Their partying had been in the papers, at first in scrapes about underage drinking, more recently when Barbara, a Yale senior, had been photographed by the tabloids dirty-dancing with a 25-year-old Ecuadoran playboy who had a few outstanding arrest warrants. Barbara was hanging off his leg. "Like a dangling chad," observed the New York *Daily News*. The girls ultimately decided to do a fashion shoot in ball gowns with *Vogue* magazine.

Bush-Cheney campaign manager Ken Mehlman was piloting his black Audi A4 home from the airport when he heard the otherworldly scream. He was giving Communications Director Nicolle Devenish a lift, and they were listening to the results of the Iowa caucuses. Howard Dean had just finished giving his concession speech/pep talk when he let loose with a primal yowl. "Holy s—t!" cried Devenish. "Listen to that guy!" Mehlman exclaimed, "He's going crazy!" Across the Potomac River at Bush-Cheney headquarters in Arlington, Va., Sara Taylor, the deputy strategy chief, was watching TV in her office. She cried out, "He just went crazy!" Adman Mark McKinnon realized that the former Vermont governor had just made the most amazing contribution to the Bush-Cheney collection of Dean speech clips, the file entitled "Dean Unplugged." Sadly, he knew it was also the last, and that the collection was now worthless. "Stick a fork in him," McKinnon told himself.

ONLY ROVE HELD OUT HOPE. Dean still had an organization, said Rove, who placed great weight on organization. Bush, who knew Dean's volatility from working with him as a fellow governor, had always suspected he would flame out. Now Bush needled his political guru about his hamburger wagers. Want to double your bets? the president asked. Dean still has money, Rove grumbled. Lots of candidates lose Iowa and come back. "This guy ain't coming back," Bush said, laughing.

Five nights later, on Jan. 24, Bush and a few of his political advisers lounged on couches in the West Sitting Hall, a living-room space in the residence with an elegant fan window. Bush was sitting in an armchair, sipping a non-alcoholic beer. He was dressed in a tuxedo and cowboy boots; later that evening he would make a few jokes at the Alfalfa Club dinner, an annual, mostly male gathering of Washington movers and shakers. Barbara and some Yale friends were wandering around. Barney, Bush's terrier, was asleep on a couch.

The mood was mellow. To be sure, the politicos arrayed on the couches, Mehlman and McKinnon and top moneyman Reynolds, were sorry to lose Dean. Mehlman remarked that Dean didn't have any money left. "I thought he was supposed to have lots of money," said Bush. The others shrugged.

They wondered: where did all the money go? Landon Parvin, a speechwriter who had been brought in to write Bush's jokes, didn't have the sense that the men in the room were particularly worried about John Kerry. Someone pointed to Kerry's long Senate record, rich with liberal votes and flip-flops. Someone else took a swipe at Teresa Heinz Kerry. She won't play well on TV, the man said. Parvin threw out a question: whom would they not like to see on the ticket as the vice presidential candidate? Bush said it didn't really matter. Lloyd Bentsen, the popular Texas senator who ran with Michael Dukakis in 1988, hadn't helped much in his own home state, said Bush.

Not everyone was so sanguine about the shape of the race. Other politicians had underestimated Kerry, the pundits and professionals kept warning. Bush would be foolish to make the same mistake. Around Washington, the Wise Men began muttering about the lack of a clear message from the Bush White House. A low but steady whine could be heard from the permanent Republican establishment, the ghosts of GOP administrations past—men who had worked for Nixon, Reagan and Bush's father, "41," as he was known (the 41st president; George W. Bush was "43," the 43rd president). President Bush boasted that he never read the newspapers, but these gray-haired ex cabinet secretaries and former top advisers, most of whom had become consultants and lawyers and lobbyists, inhaled *The New York Times* and *The Washington Post* over breakfast and listened to NPR or the off-color but clever radio talk show "Imus in the Morning" on the way to work. They were creatures of the old mainline media, which was, out of "liberal bias" or just straight reporting, growing increasingly skeptical about the Bush presidency. Over lunch at the Metropolitan Club or up at the expense-account eateries on Capitol Hill, they wondered aloud: where was Karen Hughes when the president needed her?

OVER 6 FEET TALL, with frosted hair and a strong, flat Texas accent, Hughes had been the chief message maker and enforcer in the 2000 campaign and for the first two years of the Bush presidency. Then she had retreated to Texas to be able to spend more time with her teenage son, who had loathed living in Washington. Hughes had a knack for parroting Bush's tone and voice, for "channeling" him. She also softened his hard edges. In 2000 Hughes had gently prodded Bush to play the "compassionate conservative." After she left, the Bush watchers detected a hardening in the Bush line, which they attributed to Rove, who was always reaching out to the party's true believers. Hughes had jockeyed some with Rove for power, but by and large the two forceful figures had produced a consistent message (helped by a boss who insisted on staying "on message"). Hughes had policed the wayward and zipped loose lips. When she was communications director, talking out of line would earn you "a size 11 shoe up your a—," according to a former White House official. Journalists were awed by her industrial-strength spin and no-prisoners approach to the chaos of the White House press room. They had nicknamed her Nurse Ratched, after the iron woman who ran the psycho ward in *One Flew Over the Cuckoo's Nest.*

From her home in Austin, Hughes still weighed in on key speeches and decisions, but there was no one with quite her clout running the White House communications operation. Her successor, Dan Bartlett, a former Future Farmer of America, had gone to work for Rove at the age of 22. He was regarded as "too much Karl," and hence "political." It may seem obvious that the communications director would be political, but in Bushworld advisers were supposed to stay in their lanes. The White House "message" was not just political; indeed, the leader of the free world did not want to be seen as a poll-watching politico. Rove was thought by some White House staffers to have a bit of a tin ear, to lean too hard, to reach too far to cater to his prized right-wing base. (Even Bush would crack, "That idea's so f—ing bad it sounds like something Rove came up with.")

Indeed, no one seemed to know who was in charge of the message. Rove? Bartlett? Hughes from the shadows? Bush himself? Obsessed with message discipline, the president would blow up about leaks. "I'm p—ed," he told his staff when word leaked out that he was planning to roll back steel tariffs, imposed in 2002 to give an economic lift to manufacturing (and key swing) states like Pennsylvania and West Virginia. What, exactly, was the White House message? Was the tone supposed to be cautious or bold, funny or serious? Nobody seemed to know for sure. The various admen hired by the campaign made fun of the ponderous, research-driven, tone-deaf messages handed down from on high. One original Bush-Cheney slogan was supposed to be "President Bush: Because the Stakes Are So High." The ad guy's circulated an e-mail mocking the slogan as "President Bush: Because the Steaks Are on the Grill." The slogan was quickly dropped.

It was Mark McKinnon's job to figure out how to sell Bush. McKinnon was the BC04 media man, in charge of the air war, the multimillion-dollar campaign to build Bush up and tear Kerry down. McKinnon was a bit of a misfit at the anonymous, faceless Bush-Cheney headquarters in Arlington. (To avoid truck bombs, the campaign had chosen a building set well back from the street; no sign marked the door.) The BC04 offices could have been occupied by an insurance company: rows of cubicles filled with tidy people. The dress code was by and large Brooks Brothers drab, though there did seem to be an unusual number of young blond women whose trust funds financed snappy or discreetly elegant wardrobes.

McKinnon framed his office doorway with twinkling lights. Inside he placed a Lava lamp and short, squat candles. He wore red blazers and cowboy hats. His advertising team joked that he had "metrosexual moments." Matthew Dowd, the campaign's pollster and McKinnon's partner in the "Strategery Department" (named after a late-night comedy show's parody of President Bush mangling the word "strategy"), was also a little out of place in such a button-down, fixed-smile environment. The Yeats-quoting Dowd was a chronic pessimist. (Taped to his office wall was Dowd's favorite Yeats quote: "Being Irish, he had an abiding sense of tragedy which sustained him through temporary periods of joy.") Unlike the suits all around him, Dowd usually wore cargo pants. The mood at Bush-Cheney headquarters was supposed to be relentlessly upbeat, in a corporate sort of way. Some aides noticed that unfavorable newspaper stories seemed to be omitted from the package of news clips distributed around the office. The correct mood was ordained by King Karl. "Fabulous," Rove always said, when asked how things were going. "Everything's fabulous." Oddballs, particularly artsy ones, felt a little insecure. (When deputy campaign manager Mark Wallace listed an obscure architecture book as his favorite on a media questionnaire, his girlfriend, communications director Devenish, scolded, "Honey, you can't put this down!" He filled in *Bush at War* instead.)

Dowd was a little melancholy and normally laid-back. McKinnon called him the "Valium" of the campaign. He stood in stark contrast to Ken Mehlman, the campaign manager, who was so wound up his lip trembled. His head bursting with arcane statistics (the staff called him Rain Man, after the Tom Cruise movie), Mehlman prided himself in efficiency and low overhead. He wanted to minimize the "burn rate" for campaign funds. The ad boys were always squawking that their ad budgets were being cut and their expense accounts scrutinized.

For THE FIRST BIG AD BUY in March, Dowd wanted to showcase Bush displaying true grit. McKinnon believed that voters wanted a story line, an arc, that would portray the president struggling with and overcoming adversity. Dowd focus-grouped an ad, called "Safer, Stronger," that depicted grim images, including firefighters carrying a flag-draped coffin. "When you talk about a 'day of tragedy,' the dials just go boom!" said McKinnon, throwing his hand in the air.

But convincing the Bushes took some doing. In late February, Bush invited his campaign inner circle to the White House residence for the first preview of their coming advertising assault. Bush, Rove, Bartlett and Laura Bush were all there. McKinnon was nervous. "It's like opening on Broadway," he later said. The Democratic race had shifted at warp speed. All the anti-Dean ads were out the window. Alex Castellanos, a veteran adman, had written a particularly effective one, showing an empty chair in the Oval Office and subtly raising the question of whether Dean belonged there. But Kerry did seem presidential. The Bush campaign wasn't ready to bash Kerry—yet. First they needed to run a few spots building up their own man.

There wasn't much time to work if the president was displeased with what McKinnon and Dowd had to offer. The screening, technologically speaking, was a disaster. Fumbling with the DVD machine, McKinnon kept bringing up the wrong spot, and he couldn't shut off the background music when it failed to suit the ad on the screen. The basic message of the first ad was "Safer, Stronger," but Bush worried it was too pessimistic. It opened by talking about a poor stock market and the ravages of 9/11. A second ad, "Tested," echoed similar themes and ended with a shot of the charred World Trade Center. These were not problems of Bush's creation; nonetheless, he was concerned about the somber tone. Bush was determined to be positive, upbeat. For a moment his advisers feared that they would have to scrap "Safer, Stronger." But Bush backed off, and with a few small tweaks the 9/11 ads were greenlighted.

The ads, when they were first screened on March 3, caused a dust-up. Reporters fired questions at Mehlman and the others at Bush-Cheney headquarters. Wouldn't some voters think the campaign was exploiting 9/11? Wasn't the coffin a little much? By the next day some 9/11 widows were criticizing the spots. The mainstream press turned harshly critical. BUSH CAMPAIGNS AMID A FUROR OVER ADS, read the headline in *The New York Times*. A 'SHOCKING' STUMBLE was *Newsweek*'s headline.

McKinnon and Dowd were ecstatic. At a strategy meeting the next day—the same morning the *Times* headline appeared—they joked about how they could fan the flames. Controversy sells, they said. It meant lots of "free media"; the ads were shown over and over again on news shows, particularly on cable TV. The "visual" of the rubble at the World Trade Center was a powerful reminder of the nation's darkest hour—and Bush's finest, when he climbed on the rock pile with a bullhorn. What's more, the story eclipsed some grim economic news, low job-creation numbers released by the Labor Department. McKinnon and Dowd had commiserated over the job report in Dowd's office. They knew that the strength of the economy would be the best single predictor of the election's outcome. "That was a moment when we kind of gulped and said, 'Oh, man,'" McKinnon later recalled.

At that Saturday's Breakfast Club, they were still laughing about the ad flap. (Rove had cooked eggs, bacon and some tasty venison sausage.) Dowd told the group they had received $6 million to $7 million worth of free ad coverage. "Unfortunately, we've been talking about 9/11 and our ads for five days," Dowd deadpanned at a senior staff meeting. "We're going to try to pivot back to the economy as soon as we can."

There were chuckles all around. But the group was already feeling ground down. The press coverage seemed unusually intense for such an early stage of the campaign. Ken Mehlman thought it felt like October, and it was still March. Shortly after the ads hit the air, McKinnon stopped in at Nicolle Devenish's office to find her shivering, sweating and wrapped in a blanket. McKinnon walked into Dowd's office. The lights were off. He glanced down and found Dowd asleep on the floor, passed out cold. "We're gonna kill everybody by June," McKinnon thought to himself.

THREE

"The Interregnum": Trench Warfare

After the primaries, Kerry was cranky
and his campaign began to drift.
The Bush war room wanted to "define" him,
and knew how to get under his skin.

JOHN KERRY WAS REALLY ILL. In November he had picked up a cold, the ubiquitous campaign grippe, and by February he had walking pneumonia. He had lost his voice. He looked even gaunter than usual; Lincolnesque, maybe, but he was losing weight and he couldn't sleep. A week after the New Hampshire primary, while campaigning in Kansas City, Mo., he went back to the holding room after an event and lay on the conference table. "I'm really sick," he said. He couldn't seem to get up, making his staff very nervous. "I just want to lie here for a few minutes," he croaked. But then he got up, as he always did. When Teresa was on the road with Kerry, she fussed over her husband,

Self-improved: When Teresa spoke, he was less defensive and listened

recommending various cures and soothing potions. "Sometimes my mom is very happy when John is sick because she gets to brood over him," said Teresa's son Chris Heinz. But Teresa did not like to campaign constantly with her husband, and she had her own duties running the multimillion-dollar Heinz Family Philanthropies.

Campaigning can energize a natural politician, like Bill Clinton, who feeds off crowds and sucks up adulation. For the more solitary, shy Kerry, campaigning—the day-in, day-out grind of meeting and greeting and staying "on"—was always a labor, sometimes an ordeal. Kerry's best friend from Yale, David Thorne, his former brother-in-law who had stayed close even after Kerry's divorce from Julia Thorne in 1988, worried about the toll on the candidate. The campaign was "depleting" Kerry, Thorne believed. His old friend was stoic and dogged, and Kerry rallied under pressure, but there was never enough time to truly recover. (After the campaign, Kerry insisted to *Newsweek*, "I loved campaigning. I did seven, eight events a day. I never left until I had shaken every hand.")

Kerry could be cranky. He was not a petty tyrant, like some bosses. He could be generous to his staff, who stayed loyal to him. But "he will whine constantly," said one top aide, quoting Kerry's bouts of petulance: "'I'm not getting enough exercise, I'm overscheduled, I didn't get the speech on time'—on and on, ad nauseam." Kerry's campaign manager, Mary Beth Cahill, didn't put up with much. "She cuts it off," said this aide. "She'll say, 'It wasn't anybody's fault,' or 'Whose fault was that?'" Kerry's personal aide, Marvin

Nicholson, had to grin and bear it. Kerry had met Nichol-son, 33, at a windsurfing shop in Cambridge, Mass., where Nicholson was working; he later caddied for Kerry at the Nantucket Golf Club. Now the 6-foot-8 University of West-ern Ontario grad was, in effect, his valet, serving his per-sonal needs. The two men were close friends, but Nicholson was still the servant.

The morning after the Feb. 3 primaries, which vaulted Kerry into a virtually insurmountable lead, the candidate was fuming over his missing hairbrush. He and his aides were riding in a van on the way to a *Time* magazine cover-photo shoot. Nicholson had left the hairbrush behind. "Sir, I don't have it," he said, after rummaging in the bags. "Marvin, f—!" Kerry said. The press secretary, David Wade, offered his brush. "I'm not using Wade's brush," the long-faced senator pouted. "Marvin, f—, it's my *Time* photo shoot."

Nicholson was having a bad day. Breakfast had been late and rushed and not quite right for the senator. In the van, Kerry was working his cell phone and heard the beep signal-ing that the phone was running out of juice. "Marvin, charger," he said without turning around. "Sorry, I don't have it," said Nicholson, who was sitting in the rear of the van. Now Kerry turned around. "I'm running this campaign myself," he said, looking at Nicholson and the other aides. "I get myself breakfast. I get myself hairbrushes. I get myself my cell-phone charger. It's pretty amazing." In silent frustra-tion, Nicholson helplessly punched the car seat.

The headlines that winter were mostly good, as Kerry racked up one primary victory after another. But there were some bumps and one near miss. On Feb. 12 Matt Drudge, the Internet gossip columnist, reported that two major news organizations were working on a story that Kerry had an "intern problem" with a young female campaign worker. The story was bogus, but in the post–Monica Lewinsky era, the Kerry campaign feared it would break out of the cesspool of the lower tabloids and Drudge and make it into the mainstream press, cause a distracting flap and possibly open the door to a late Edwards challenge. Democratic members of Congress, whose staffs read Drudge like everyone else in the Washington journalist-politico world, were anxiously calling in to Kerry headquarters. Kerry's staff had to feverishly work the phones to newspaper reporters, imploring and bluffing and trying to play on what little shame the press had left. "No one else is doing it. You'd be the only one," the Kerry staffers would say to the reporters and pray that they were telling the truth. The *New York Post* came closest to running with the story but backed off. The damage was contained; it turned out to be the usual confection of false rumors, possibly stirred up by troublemaking staffers from rival camps.

On March 2 Kerry swept the last big slew of primaries, and Senator Edwards, who had been waging a spirited if futile race, finally conceded. On the campaign trail Kerry ran chronically late. He did not like to be "handled," and when advance men rushed him, he gave them a "back off" look and proceeded at his own deliberate pace. On the night of the Feb. 3 primaries, Kerry had taken so long to get to the cameras to declare victory that he had permitted Edwards to dominate the airwaves. His chief strategist, Bob Shrum, had ranted and raved that Kerry was going to miss the Eastern media markets altogether if he didn't get onstage any faster.

Bᴜᴛ ᴡɪᴛʜ ᴛʜᴇ ʀᴀᴄᴇ ᴏᴠᴇʀ, Kerry was suddenly thrust into the bubble of the Secret Service, which was charged with protecting the Democratic nominee. The Secret Service was usually able to make anyone, with the possible exception of Bill Clinton, run on time, in part because its agents could literally stop traffic. So on the night of March 2 it was a thrill and a relief for the family entourage to be able to roar downtown from Teresa's house in Georgetown to a victory celebration at the Old Post Office Pavilion on Pennsylvania Avenue in just seven minutes, sirens whooping, lights flashing. Whispering into their cuffs, the Secret Service agents rushed the presumptive nominee into the elevator and everyone piled in for the ascent to the main hall, one story up.

The elevator rose half a floor and abruptly stopped. The increasingly agitated agents and advance men began loudly whispering into their sleeves again. One agent fruitlessly tried to wedge the door open. The heat rose. Kerry's stepson Chris Heinz and his two daughters, Vanessa and Alexandra, tried to crack jokes. The candidate sat down on the floor, rested his forehead on his arms and went into a silent trance. Heinz looked down at his stepfather. "You OK down there?" he asked. The senator tersely replied, "Heat rises."

After 15 minutes of increasingly hot and claustrophobic waiting, a technician arrived, the door was pried open, an advance man climbed out and the elevator—lighter now—began to rise again. The doors opened. Kerry looked out at the waiting crowd. "Let's not take that elevator again," he said coolly. Everyone chuckled, nervously.

On the drive back to Georgetown, the motorcade raced south of the White House on Constitution Avenue. Vanessa Kerry could see the White House ablaze in light, the tantalizing prize—now, incredibly, within her father's reach. She and Alex felt moved, overwhelmed, but noticed that their father didn't. Within a couple of minutes of delivering his victory speech he had been back on his cell phone. "Dad," said Alex, who is close to her father and direct with him, "will you please appreciate this moment for 10 seconds?" He mumbled, yes, yes, he was happy, it was good, and then went back to working the cell phone, trying to find aides to line up fund-raising events. It occurred to Vanessa that the cliché was wrong; her father was not, as the scribes would say, a fourth-quarter player, he was a marathon man. Kerry liked to say that "every day is extra" after Vietnam, but actually every day was like the day before, a relentless march toward his goal.

The period between the last primary and the summer conventions is an odd time in presidential campaigns. In earlier campaigns it had been the political equivalent of the "phony war," the long, strange lull in fighting in World War II between the Nazi invasion of Poland in September 1939 and the blitzkrieg through Europe in the spring of 1940. This time around, there would be no phony war. The polarized electorate, the constant chatter on talk radio and cable TV, the frenetic pace of campaigning by the candidates, gave the campaign a truly warlike feel in the spring of 2004. A better comparison was World War I: trench warfare, muddy and gassy, with neither side able to secure much ground and keep it.

The Kerry campaign was well aware of the importance of maintaining momentum, of not easing off after the primaries and allowing the Bush campaign to dominate. In 2000, the Gore campaign had been listless all spring while George W. Bush was convincing voters that he was really a "compassionate conservative." At least money would not be a problem this time around. Kerry had only about $2 million in cash on March 1 (versus more than $100 million in the Bush coffers), but raising money was proving to be easy, thanks partly to the intensity of anti-Bush feeling. By forcing Kerry to "bust the caps" and go outside the campaign-finance system, Howard Dean had done the Democrats a great favor. Al Gore had spent only about $9 million during the 2000 phony war; Kerry planned to spend more like $80 million. Kerry had genuine momentum coming out of the primaries. This was the time to capitalize on it and fix in the voters' minds the image of the Democratic candidate as a thoughtful war hero, a man who didn't just shoot from the hip but was strong enough to come from behind.

On March 8 top aides gathered for a strategy session in Bob Shrum's well-appointed, airy office overlooking the Potomac. Tad Devine, Shrum's partner and a key strategist, stressed, "We can't let down and relax." It was important, he said, for Kerry to recover from his chronic cold, but after a little rest he needed to be out on the trail. Devine called the period between the primaries and the convention "the interregnum," and proposed what he called an "ideas primary." Kerry would offer his solutions to the pressing problems of the day: getting the economy going again and restoring international faith in American foreign policy.

Kerry was soon out speaking about jobs and education, the environment and mending relations with the allies, but he wasn't connecting. Part of his problem was Iraq, which was veering out of control, with uprisings and bombings and kidnappings. Kerry was curiously mute on the crisis. He could urge greater international involvement, but with Iraq still in chaos, why would foreign countries send people who might just be taken hostage? So Kerry mostly talked about doing the responsible thing and staying the course, which was about what Bush was already doing.

The real problem was not the subject but the speaker. Kerry's friend Sen. Joe Biden, ranking Democrat on the Foreign Relations Committee, was far more animated on the Sunday talk shows, comparing the Iraqi uprisings that spring to the Tet Offensive in Vietnam in 1968. There was something soporific about Kerry's style that made his speeches, no matter how considered and reasonable, seem forgettable.

Not surprisingly, the press seemed to pay more attention to Kerry's occasional testy outbursts. At the end of March he went skiing, an essential outlet for a man who uses vigorous, high-stress sports as a release. "Unbelievable—I didn't think about the campaign the whole time I was up there," he exulted after one particularly grueling day in the northern

Rockies of Sun Valley, Idaho, where Teresa kept one of her five houses. Kerry was happy to be slogging up mountains and snowboarding down icy chutes, but he collided with a clumsy Secret Service man and told him off in crude language. A couple of reporters, from ABC and *The Boston Globe,* were skiing nearby and publicized the incident. Then on "Good Morning America" in early April, the candidate bridled when the normally genial host Charlie Gibson asked him about an old controversy, recently brought back to life by Vice President Dick Cheney and other Bush surrogates, over whether Kerry had thrown away his medals (or just his ribbons) at an antiwar protest in 1971. Kerry was indignant about having his honor questioned, and at the end of the interview, with the camera still rolling, he snapped at Gibson, "Thanks for doing the work of the RNC [the Republican National Committee]."

O FFSTAGE, KERRY'S HANDLERS CRINGED. Putting him on first thing in the morning on an issue he cared about viscerally was a mistake, they realized. Kerry cannot deflect a question when he is wrapped up in the sureness of his position. (John Edwards, on the other hand, was able to deftly redirect the question back to Cheney's draft status during the Vietnam War. Questioned about Kerry's medals by talk-show host Don Imus, Edwards shot back with a laugh, "Five deferrals, and you're asking me about John Kerry?")

Kerry clearly needed help with his speaking skills, so in early spring he quietly appeared at the 17th Street offices of

Michael Sheehan, a well-known Washington speech coach who has helped numerous Democratic politicians—and worked with some, like Gore, who seemed beyond help. The question was whether Kerry belonged in the latter category. Sheehan told Kerry that he had to learn to shift to a more conversational style, to vary the pace, to sound more casual in his speech. Otherwise, his speeches all sounded the same and gave the impression that what he was saying was calculated—that he was thinking about what he was saying rather than saying what he felt.

Kerry was not defensive with Sheehan. Indeed, he invited criticism, as he often did. Kerry may have been reserved and aloof, but he was a self-improver, and he wanted to do whatever it took to win. With aides he would sometimes say, "Tell me everything you think I'm doing wrong." He always appeared to be listening. But was he really? Were his shortcomings as a speaker somehow hard-wired? It was hard to know.

KERRY'S BACKERS NEVER STOPPED searching for signs, for some signal that he would hear the music. In August 2003, when the campaign had been floundering and unable to raise any money, a group of Kerry's top fund-raisers met at his Beacon Hill town house. The moneymen were almost desperate. They implored him to be more aggressive, to really take on Dean. Kerry was defensive and prickly. He pushed back: Why hadn't the fund-raisers called this or that contributor? Why hadn't they reminded the contributor of all that Kerry had done for him? The fund-raisers became argumentative: Why aren't you out there more? "I have been out there," Kerry snapped. As the meeting was deteriorating into recriminations, Teresa Heinz Kerry slipped into the room, apologizing for her tardiness. She immediately took the side of the fund-raisers, telling her husband, "No, John, you haven't been aggressive enough." Kerry sparred with her, calling her "love," but insisting that he was trying harder. His mood softened; he seemed less defensive. As Teresa led a discussion of "the things we need to do better," Kerry seemed to be listening.

When they trooped out of Kerry's mansion on that steamy August night, the moneymen had felt a sense of relief, even optimism. At least Teresa was serious about turning the campaign around. And indeed Kerry's campaigning did improve. But it took him two months to get going. And then, after he had won the nomination, he seemed to fall back into dull Senate speak.

It was almost taken for granted around the Bush-Cheney campaign that "going negative" against Kerry was the way to go. "It's a no-brainer, it's just sort of campaigning 101," said adman Mark McKinnon. Despite his string of primary wins, Kerry was still not well known to the American people. The BC04 team wanted to use a good chunk of their $150 million–plus war chest to "define" Kerry—that is, to paint him as a tax-hiking, flip-flopping liberal. On March 11, just a week after the Bush campaign had begun to build up the president with "positive" ads, including the so-called 9/11 spots, the team began buying ads in key swing states imagining Kerry's first 100 days in office. By plumbing—and twisting and exaggerating—his old Senate voting record, they were able to make him look like a profligate supporter of big government. In one ad titled "Wacky," McKinnon's ad team suggested that Kerry would raise gasoline taxes by 50 cents.

Negative advertising is only one brushstroke in the dark arts of modern campaigning. All major campaigns maintain "rapid response" units. The 24/7 media and the technology of the Internet demand it. A campaign can no longer spend the day working for that one good 90-second "visual" on the evening news. On cable TV the message of the day can lock in early, getting repeated every half hour or so unless it is successfully rebutted or trumped. The first state-of-the-art rapid-response unit was set up by Bill Clinton's top political operatives, James Carville and George Stephanopoulos, back in 1992. Viewed today, the cult-film documentary from that campaign, *The War Room,* with its clunky mobile phones and fax machines, might as well be a remnant from the silent-screen era. Technology has quickened the pace and provided new weapons for hitting back. Digital video-recording devices can "capture" an image of a candidate making a speech and immediately pass it around via e-mail and the Internet. Admen can cut a response ad overnight, if not sooner.

IT TAKES A CERTAIN BREED of sleepless media junkie with a jugular instinct to run a good war room. The director of rapid response for the Bush-Cheney campaign, Steve

Schmidt, fit the part. Chunky, with a shiny bald head, he looked like an artillery shell. When he talked, his small blue eyes darted around the room at the flickering TV sets. As he spouted rapid-fire talking points, sometimes a hint of a crooked smile would creep across his lips, as if he pitied anyone on the receiving end of such a high-velocity, hard-hammering spin machine. Schmidt liked to refer to himself as Patton. His staff called him the General or the Colonel. His aides described him stalking through the halls of the headquarters declaring, "Kill, kill, kill!" They were not sure how much he was kidding. (After the election, Schmidt insisted that he never said "Kill, kill, kill!" or compared himself to Gen. Patton. "That's not how I comport myself," he said. "War and politics are not the same thing. This makes me look like a dickhead. I did insist on precision and that people be on time. There was joking, of course. I didn't go around looking like a tin horn dictator.")

Smart campaigns, even ones with more than $100 million to spend on destroying an opponent, do not just use brute force. Clever operatives know how to practice jujitsu, to use their opponent's strength against him. Kerry was a deliberate and thoughtful man, but his need to constantly explain himself was a weakness, and not just because it bored people. Kerry was reactive. Properly baited, he could be led into a trap that was partly of his own creation.

The Bush-Cheney campaign knew about Kerry's vulnerability from the outset. "If the rabbit runs, he'll chase it," said campaign manager Ken Mehlman. Possibly, Mehlman thought, Kerry had overlearned the lesson of the 1988 campaign, when Democratic candidate Michael Dukakis was sluggish about responding to the barbs and provocations of the Republican dirty tricksters. But Mehlman and the others didn't realize, at first, just how self-defeating Kerry's rational process could be. As a matter of routine, the Bush operatives tried to goad Kerry. And when he reacted, they were ready.

In the third week of March, the BC04 team learned, Kerry was headed to West Virginia to talk about national security. The Mountain State was a critical swing state, full of veterans who could go either way. (By summer Bush was spending so much time there, his advisers were joking that their unofficial slogan was "If it's Sunday, it's West Virginia!") On Monday, March 15, McKinnon's team repaired to his ad shop, Maverick Media, to crank out a spot that would air on the West Virginia airwaves just in time to greet Kerry. In the ad, a grave baritone voice intones, "Mr. Kerry?" calling on the senator to cast his vote for or against more funding for the troops in Iraq. Kerry appears to vote no again and again (in fact, it was a single vote). At 7 the next morning the ad was digitally whisked to West Virginia, where it began playing on local TV.

That noon, when Kerry addressed a veterans group in West Virginia, a heckler kept demanding to know why he had voted against more funding for the troops. In his considered but long-winded fashion, Kerry tried to explain that he had wanted to vote for the funding, but only if the Senate passed an amendment that would whittle down President Bush's earlier tax cut for the rich. Kerry voted for the amendment, but when it failed, he voted against the funding. The heckler pressed, and Kerry, losing patience, fell into senatorial procedural shorthand. "I actually did vote for the $87 billion before I voted against it," he said.

At Bush-Cheney headquarters, Joe Kildae, a 25-year-old campaign intern who monitored the war room (and never seemed to sleep), was watching. In his cubicle he kept three televisions and a battery of TiVos and VCRs. As soon as he saw Kerry make his remark on Fox News, he stood up in his cubicle and caught the eye of his boss, Steve Schmidt. Schmidt had seen the clip, too. The two men nodded at each other. Kildae thought to himself: "We're going to be seeing this a lot." He immediately hit pause on his digital recorder, wound the clip back and copied it to tape. Using a program called TVEyes, he pulled up an instant rough transcript. He e-mailed the transcript of Kerry's "flip-flopping" to an "alert list" of top aides, who could then click on a link to see the video.

"You gotta see this," Kildae told campaign communications adviser Terry Holt. "Oh, my God," Holt replied. "You have to send that to me on my BlackBerry." The video of Kerry's shooting himself in the foot flew around Bush-Cheney headquarters and, very soon, into the hungry ether beyond.

McKinnon and his ad team wasted no time. "The second we saw it, we knew we had a new ad," McKinnon later recalled. "The greatest gifts in politics are the gifts the other side gives you." It was so simple. All they had to do was drop the footage of Kerry saying "I actually did vote for the $87 billion before I voted against it" into the ad that was already running, chastising Kerry for cutting funding. McKinnon called the new ad "Troops-Fog." Much of its airing was free: news shows picked up the clip of the "flip-flop" and plastered it on screens like wallpaper.

It took a while for the Kerry campaign to even realize that its candidate had been badly wounded. Kerry himself realized he had made a mistake, but at his headquarters, most of the chatter was about the "weird heckler" who had asked him the question. The Kerry campaign would later insist that the Bush campaign had spent millions that spring to smear its candidate without much effect, but in fact Kerry's "negatives" climbed in some key swing states. Just as important, perhaps, he had missed an opportunity to define himself in a positive or memorable way. The Bush "Troops-Fog" act blew enough fog to unsettle voters, to make them wonder about Kerry's consistency and the depth of his conviction.

The Kerry campaign continued to drift, unable to break through. Kerry himself was flummoxed. Paging through a speech draft in early April, he wondered aloud, "What is our message?" Kerry's caution, his fondness for nuance and his essential sense of responsibility kept getting in the way. To the dismay of aides, he cut voter-pleasing preschool programs from his proposed domestic-spending plan because he didn't want to run up the deficit. He boned up on foreign-policy arcana for interviews—you never knew when Tim Russert might ask a question about, say, Cyprus. But he continued to say nothing remarkable about Iraq. On Capitol Hill, Democrats were panicking. Kerry's own family was hearing the bad buzz and anxiously trying to reassure themselves that "staying the course" was the way to go.

On a morning in early April, Bob Shrum seemed even edgier than usual, popping Nicorettes and spinning a conference-room chair next to him. Shrum was determined to "play our game and not the press's game," as he put it. Let the media squawk and the Republicans take the low road. The money was pouring in now—more than $50 million in the first quarter of 2004, about half of that from the Internet, the money machine discovered by Howard Dean. (In April, Kerry would outraise Bush.) There would be time to build up Kerry; in the meantime, let Bush self-destruct as his failed policies became more and more apparent.

Somehow, though, the long-awaited Bush collapse wasn't happening, at least not yet. Iraq seemed to be in flames. At a press conference in mid-April, Bush told a reporter that, try as he might, he just couldn't think of a mistake he had made since 9/11. The press and the chattering classes hooted in derision. But Bush actually went up in the polls. Most voters seemed to like the president's show of resolve. Kerry was baffled. He said with a sigh to one top staffer, "I can't believe I'm losing to this idiot."

CHRIS HEINZ, KERRY'S STEPSON, was struck late one evening in April when he found the candidate sitting silently, alone, in a vast hotel suite in San Francisco. The room was a far cry from the spare and sometimes seedy motels of January. "When did all this happen?" Heinz asked, looking around. "I don't know," said Kerry. After a pause: "I think it was around Feb. 3. Definitely March 2, the hotel rooms started getting nicer. In mid-March they put a bike in my room."

"Wow. Cool," said Heinz.

"I know," Kerry said.

The exchange was typical enough between them; the two graduates of St. Paul's and Yale had forged a boasting, joshing preppy-jock bond centered on their mutual fondness for hockey, skiing and extreme sports. Speaking in crude, macho shorthand, they could sound, at times, like boarding-school roommates who had just returned from vacation.

Heinz, who is not shy, decided to try a little "reality check" to test Kerry's true spirits.

"You know what, John?" the stepson said. "Nov. 3 is going to be f—ed up. The whole thing is going to be f—ed up."

"What do you mean?" Kerry asked.

"Well, look," Heinz said. "John, if you win, you're the president of the United States. That's pretty f—ed up."

Kerry, smiling, nodded tentatively. "Yeah, all right."

"And if you lose," Heinz continued, "I'm not even going to tell you how f—ed up that is."

Kerry's cheeks, perched plump above a toothy grin, sank into an empty expression. "That's it," he said. "That's enough of that."

There were some places you didn't go with Kerry.

Mended fence: After rebuffing Kerry, McCain joined his old foe Bush on the stump (Photo by Charles Ommanney / Contact for *Newsweek*)

FOUR

Trail Mix:
Teaming Up

*The Bush campaign tried to stay
a step ahead of the bad news—
and Kerry groped for a bold stroke.*

IN LATE APRIL, Bush's top campaign operatives were feeling pretty pleased with themselves. They were crowing over Democratic polling data showing that Kerry's negative ratings had jumped 11 points in the last two months. The Democrats blamed the wave of Bush-Cheney attack ads (by the end of May, BC04 would buy 49,050 spots in the hundred top media markets; three quarters of Bush's ads were negative). True, the Democrats would have to fault the Republicans, since they couldn't very well blame their own candidate. Still, for the spinmeisters at BC04, it was gratifying to see the opposition acknowledge their good work.

Even better, the economic news was looking up for Bush. At the beginning of every month, the BC04 policy director,

Tim Adams, would be the bearer of economic tidings to the morning staff meeting. For months the job-growth numbers from the Bureau of Labor Statistics—an economic measure critical to the president's re-election hopes—were anemic. Adams had come to dread the long faces when he walked into the room. But on April 2, a hugely relieved Adams reported 308,000 jobs created in March, the best job growth in four years. Adams's hands were shaking as he read off the numbers. The room erupted in cheers. The staff meeting that day was a "laugh-a-palooza," recalled a Bush aide.

Thanks to the ineptitude of the Kerry campaign and their own nimbleness, the Bushites somehow managed to stay a step ahead of the bad news that spring—for a while, at least. The sense of smugness at BC04 couldn't last. Iraq was getting nastier by the day, and the job-growth numbers would dip again. By any measurement, President Bush had a terrible spring of 2004, a series of domestic and foreign-policy disasters that would have badly shaken most modern presidencies. But through his own willfulness, his determination never to look back and the artfulness of his handlers (who were made to look good by comparison with their foes), Bush defied the facts on the ground for as long as possible.

Reality was biting in Iraq that April. In Fallujah, rioters, prating for the cameras, strung up the burned and mutilated bodies of four Americans. In Washington and New York the chattering classes were buzzing over Bob Woodward's new book, *Plan of Attack*. The *Washington Post* reporter had gained extraordinary access to the pre-invasion deliberations of the Bush White House. It did not appear, from a careful reading of the book, that Bush's top advisers had thoroughly discussed the option of not going to war, or whether invading Iraq might do more harm than good in the war on terror. But Woodward did not spell out any critical judgments, and the book could also be read to show the president's determination. In a brilliant jujitsu move, the Bush White House decided not to try to rebut the book, but rather to embrace it. An aide—possibly Nicolle Devenish, the campaign communications director, though others credited strategist Matthew Dowd—suggested they post the book on the campaign Web site under "Suggested Reading." The strategy, said adman Mark McKinnon with a laugh, was "love the book you're with." Or, as he put it, "Let's love it to death."

OUTFOXING THE MEDIA ESTABLISHMENT was a favorite occupation of the Bush White House. Press-bashing is an old Republican sport, more so in the George W. Bush era. The president disliked press conferences. He would tease individual reporters and give them nicknames, but he disdained the press as a whole. As a young campaign operative working for his father in 1988, Bush had advised his colleagues not to bother to steer reporters away from wrong stories. He preferred to let reporters hang themselves. At press conferences, he just assumed that reporters were out to get him, and sneered at correspondents' "peacocking" for the cameras.

With the press astir over Iraq and the failure to find any weapons of mass destruction, the April 13 press conference—

only Bush's 12th since taking office, the lowest number since Ronald Reagan, who had held 23 by the same point in his presidency—promised to be contentious. White House aides informed the president that reporters were planning to "brother-in-law"—work together to follow up each other's questions. "Really?" Bush deadpanned, unimpressed. The Bush team decided, just in case the press gabble became too loud and obnoxious (or Bush lost his sang-froid under fire), to have the president open with a long statement of resolve, a kind of pre-emptive strike before the sniping began.

During the question-and-answer, Bush doggedly repeated his shows of resolve, but he seemed scratchy and petulant with reporters and absolutely refused to acknowledge that he had done anything wrong. The press panned Bush's performance, but the public did not. Less than a week later, a Gallup poll declared Bush's approval still at 52%. The late-night comics were having fun with Bushisms, but at the "Strategery Department" of BC04 headquarters, everyone was laughing along. The Bushies had adopted the "Strategery" title during the last election after comic actor Will Ferrell had made fun of Bush's malapropisms on "Saturday Night Live." Now, when Jon Stewart's "Daily Show" on Comedy Central spoofed the BC04 attack ads, everyone in Strategery chortled. In one segment, correspondent Ed Helms jokingly gushed over his favorite, the "Troops-Fog" ad that had featured Kerry's "$87 billion" gaffe. Michael Moore's *Fahrenheit 9/11* had just won top prize at the Cannes Film Festival—the Palme d'Or—and Helms used the award as a pun. "I award this ad my highest praise," he simpered. "The coveted Palme de Bitch-Slap." For McKinnon's birthday on May 5, his colleagues presented him with a small golden "Palme de Bitch-Slap" statuette. McKinnon stuck it on top of his TV.

Unlike John Kerry, George W. Bush liked to take the stump—at least he had in past campaigns. Glad-handing and joking around with an audience energized him. He shed that deer-in-the-headlights look that sometimes came over him at press conferences. Speaking in formal settings, enunciating with ponderous deliberation, as if he was terrified he might mispronounce a big word, Bush could look uneasy, stiff, muscle-bound. But on the trail, with his sleeves rolled up, bantering with audience members (all carefully selected in advance by the tight, ruthlessly efficient BC04 organization), he had often exuded a macho, good-ole-boy charm.

STILL, IT WASN'T EASY for Bush to make the switch from War President to Happy Warrior in the spring of 2004. He knew that he had to get out there, to campaign in May the way presidents usually do in October. But it took time for him to relax, to find his old groove. Marc Racicot, the former governor of Montana and chief of the RNC, a close Bush friend who was titular chairman of BC04, worried that the president's heart really wasn't in this one. It wasn't just that his hair was a little grayer or that the lines around his eyes were etched a little deeper. Bush seemed more impatient, less joyful. He wasn't having much fun. Racicot worried that Bush's prickliness would show through and undermine one of his greatest election assets, his likability. He thought that Bush needed to be a little softer and more intimate, to share more. Racicot worried about the president's mood. All winter and spring, Bush had been meeting privately with the families of soldiers who had fallen in Iraq. The meetings were described to the press in the most anodyne terms, but in fact they were searing, often tearful for the president and the families alike. They did not leave Bush much wanting to go out and grin and jape and press the flesh.

And yet he made himself do it, sitting up front in a bus shrink-wrapped in a red, white and blue shell emblazoned YES, AMERICA CAN. The bus had a plush captain's chair, a two-foot presidential seal hanging on the back wall and a 20-inch flat-screen TV. ("It's better than my apartment," cracked CBS radio correspondent Mark Knoller.) In the first week of May, President Bush hopscotched from small town to small town through the Midwest, shoring up the Republicans' rural base, which was beginning to look a little shaky. Bush was as impatient as ever; he couldn't stand windy introductions from local pols who wished to bask in their moment of reflected glory. Kept waiting, he would pace backstage "like a caged animal," said one aide. The solution: the locals were commanded to keep their introductions brief. Really brief, as in: "Ladies and gentlemen, the president of the United States!"

The last stop on the two-day tour was a rally at a hockey arena in Cincinnati. The lights dimmed, strobe lights flickered and "Eye of the Tiger," the theme song from *Rocky III,* suddenly boomed through the hall. Bush came sauntering with his famous swagger, the sheriff ready to draw into the spotlight. Some 10,000 people went wild. "I'm gonna find the person who put on this event," Bush exulted, "and give 'em a raise!" He went through his routines. *"Vamos a ganar!"* he shouted in Spanish. "That means, 'We're gonna win!'" His voice was hoarse and cracking from two days on the stump, but at last he seemed to be enjoying himself.

The euphoria was fleeting. Earlier that week "60 Minutes II" had revealed horrific abuses of Iraqi detainees at a hellhole Iraqi prison named Abu Ghraib. On May 3, while Bush was touring the rural Midwest, investigative reporter Seymour Hersh published a piece in *The New Yorker* magazine revealing a secret Pentagon report on Abu Ghraib that suggested the abuses had been sanctioned by military and CIA officers. The wretched photos spilled into the press, grotesque images of naked Iraqi men being tortured and humiliated by their American captors.

At the White House, President Bush was furious that he had not been told about the report, and his aides orchestrated a leak to all the major papers suggesting that Bush blamed Donald Rumsfeld, his headstrong Defense secretary. The press went on one of its periodic feeding frenzies: was Bush going to dump his favorite war minister? Bush was irritated by the press speculation (and the apparent glee of reporters who had finally found a crack in the war hawks' united front). On May 10, the president made a show of support for Rumsfeld, going to the Pentagon to praise him. But the troubles in Iraq were finally starting to have a political impact.

Republican pollster Ed Goeas had been watching a key sector: rural voters. They were considered part of the GOP base, but "soft" in pollspeak, vulnerable to being lured away by Kerry if they turned against the war. Combat losses in Iraq came disproportionately from rural America; at some point, the rising toll in Iraq was likely to make the mothers of dead and maimed soldiers wonder if the cost was worth it. Pollster Goeas had been relieved when support for the president in rural areas shot up after Bush's mid-April press conference. But now the numbers were trending down, not dramatically, but noticeably, by several points in many polls. Rural voters would rally around a strong president who seemed purposeful and in control. But the prison scandal, with its horrific images, and the finger-pointing and blame-ducking that followed, were dispiriting to even the most patriotic farmers and small-town dwellers. As he pored over the data in his Alexandria, Va., office in late May, Goeas wondered whether voters were beginning to ask: is anyone in charge here? For a president who was running on his strong leadership, Goeas thought, that could mean big trouble.

AT BC04 HEADQUARTERS, strategy boss and chief pollster Matthew Dowd was having the same gloomy thoughts. Dowd had known that the prison scandal would hurt with women. The corridor outside his office was decorated with a NASCAR racing poster; the area was known as Pit Row.

NASCAR fans were seen as a key swing vote—not so much the men, who were mostly pro-Bush, but the women (roughly 40 percent of NASCAR fans are female), who were more likely to be on the fence. Dowd fretted that men and women alike were drifting away from Bush, discouraged by the steady drumbeat of bad news from Iraq and Bush's apparent inability to get a handle on the crisis.

The mood at BC04 seemed down as the torpor of early summer settled over Washington. A feeling of ennui, of going through the motions, even of paralysis, seemed to be infecting Bush headquarters. For the first time, people were beginning to whisper that Bush might actually lose the election. Pessimism was heresy in Bushland—the relentlessly upbeat Karl Rove wouldn't hear of it. But BC04 staffers were beginning to confess to each other, though not very loudly, their qualms. They began to have impermissible feelings of unease and defeatism. "Everyone just had that feeling within themselves," a Bushite told a *Newsweek* reporter in June. She said it quietly.

Bush's speechwriters were struggling to strike just the right balance. Michael Gerson, Bush's talented wordsmith, understood that sunny Reaganisms would fall flat, that it was not exactly Morning in America for most people. On the other hand, the president did not want to sound downbeat. The calibrations became ever more minute. The day before each speech, Rove, who was a human Geiger counter when it came to detecting underlying voting trends, state by state, precinct by precinct, would sit down with Gerson to discuss just the right word choice, depending on the audience—

where and when to sound empathetic, where and when to be more positive.

The balancing act became slightly ludicrous. The campaign had begun to resort to gimmicks to smooth over bad economic news. Bush's aides began to police hot-button words that didn't test well. Bush speechwriters would roll their eyes when Communications Director Dan Bartlett or another higher-up suggested a certain word to avoid. One was "competition," because "people are unnerved by talk of competition," a Bush aide explained. "It sounds too strenuous and difficult." The speechwriters would abide by the rules for a few weeks and then ignore them.

Mark McKinnon, the campaign's ad guru, was feeling thwarted. He thought the campaign was on autopilot. The attack ads on Kerry no longer seemed to be working. He thought there were some promising things happening in Iraq under the media radar, but the bad news was overshadowing everything. McKinnon had become fascinated with former pro-football player Pat Tillman, who had gone into the Army and been killed (by his own troops in a friendly-fire accident) in Afghanistan. McKinnon was overcome by Tillman's humility and sacrifice. The BC04 director of paid media had even gone to a tattoo parlor to have Tillman's jersey number, 40, etched in black ink on his right shoulder. McKinnon needed a break. He had been forced to cancel a family vacation earlier that spring; in the first week of June, during a campaign lull while the nation mourned the death of President Reagan, he packed up his family and flew off for 10 days to Sydney, Australia.

In the 1960 presidential campaign, Theodore White, author of *The Making of the President,* began noticing that teeny-boppers and young children (and not a few housewives) were bobbing up and down as John F. Kennedy's motorcade sped by. White called them "Jumpers." By 2004, there weren't many Jumpers for George W. Bush. But in the generally supportive audiences that lined the roads, there were some Downers, mostly solitary elderly people who would look up with sour faces and then thrust their thumbs down as Bush's bus passed by. There were even some Double Downers, who would use both thumbs to express themselves. On July 9, Bush flew to Allentown, Pa. The countryside was leafy and green, the day was sunny and bright, but as the motorcade passed, old person after old person contorted their faces into frowns and gave the thumbs-down sign. One spectator, maybe a Kerry plant, maybe just a citizen afflicted with That Feeling, held up a handmade sign. It read: I FEEL SICK.

BUSH WAS SLOWLY SINKING in the polls, but somehow Kerry didn't appear to be getting much of a lift. The Democratic candidate seemed incapable of exploiting Bush's liabilities. Kerry, the two-decade member of the Senate Foreign Relations Committee, was trying to sell his depth of knowledge and worldliness, yet he remained tongue-tied on the overarching foreign-policy crisis of the day, the mess in Iraq. (After the election, Kerry disputed this characterization. "I had laid out five specific speeches on Iraq. The problem was the media," he said.) Other global hot spots were untouchable. On NBC's "Meet the Press," Tim Russert asked Kerry if he agreed with Bush's policy toward Israel. The normally loquacious, nuanced Kerry had a one-word answer: "Yes." The Kerry campaign had heard that Karl Rove was waging a whispering campaign in the Miami condos that Kerry was weak on Israel. Kerry was very skittish about offending elderly Jewish voters, who turned out in droves in one of the most critical swing states.

Kerry was still unable to come up with an all-encompassing theme or message, a memorable way of explaining why he was running. His intellectualism and fussiness got in the way. When speechwriters wrote in pithy lines, Kerry would cross them out. "It sounds so slogany," he would say. Kerry hated to repeat himself, a serious drawback for a politician (Bush could repeat the same lines, over and over). At one point, Kerry did fasten on to a line from a Langston Hughes poem, "Let America Be America Again." It sounded uplifting, at least to Kerry. But voters, who by and large had never heard of Hughes, were confused; some of them were even offended. Was Kerry saying that supporting Bush was un-American? Kerry dropped the line.

In July, the Kerry campaign decided that the Democrats couldn't afford to cede the "values" issue to the Republicans. In a speech in Cloquet, Minn., Kerry waxed on about "values that are rooted in the heartland" and laid claim to "conservative values" himself. But a week later, at a fund-raiser in New York, he went onstage after some Hollywood stars had made vulgar jokes about the president and proclaimed,

"Every single performer" in the program "conveyed to you the heart and soul of our country." This was too rich for the Bush campaign, always on the alert for Kerry flip-flops (a sign on the door of Communications Director Devenish read, IT'S THE HYPOCRISY, STUPID). Did Kerry really mean that Whoopi Goldberg's crude humor represented "conservative values"? In a not-so-subtle reminder of who truly owned heartland values, Bush began campaigning around the Midwest with HEART AND SOUL OF AMERICA banners.

Kerry's closest friends and family were worried. "Too much senatese," Sen. Edward Kennedy scolded him in May. Kerry's daughter Alex, a filmmaker, often critiqued her father's wooden TV performances—so much so that she began to worry that her criticism was coloring her relationship with her father. It seemed, she fretted, that their conversations consisted of "I saw you on TV, you need to try this differently, you have to fix this." In June, Alex ran into filmmaker Steven Spielberg in Los Angeles and voiced her concerns. "If I give you $5," she implored Spielberg, only half-kidding, "will you please try to get through to my dad about this thing? Maybe he'll listen to you."

Kerry was too cautious, too set in his ways, to fundamentally change his speech patterns and delivery. But in one important area, he was willing—even desperate—to try something bold. He badly wanted Sen. John McCain to be his running mate. As far back as August 2003, Kerry had taken McCain to breakfast to sound him out: would the maverick Republican run on a unity ticket with Kerry? In the mid-'90s, the two Vietnam combat vets had forged a friendship, a brotherhood, while trying to calm down veterans groups obsessed over rumors about POWs and MIAs still alive in Vietnam. Kerry knew that McCain was still bitter over the dirty tricks played on him during the 2000 campaign by Bush mudslingers, who spread rumors that McCain had fathered a black child by a prostitute. Here was a chance for payback against Bush that would change history—not just a chance to get even, but much more grandly an opportunity to bridge the Red State/Blue State divide, break the Washington logjam and bring the country together.

McCain batted away the idea as not serious. But Kerry was intent, and after he wrapped up the nomination in March, he went back after McCain a half-dozen more times. "I can't say this is an offer because I've got to be able to deny it," Kerry told his friend. "But you've got to do this." To show just how sincere he was, he made an outlandish offer. If McCain said yes, he would expand the role of vice president to include Secretary of Defense and the overall control of foreign policy. (The deal was reminiscent of the so-called co-presidency offered to Gerald Ford by Ronald Reagan at the 1980 Republican convention; the suggestion fell apart of its own weight.) McCain exclaimed, "You're out of your mind. I don't even know if it's constitutional, and it certainly wouldn't sell."

That meant no. Kerry was thwarted and furious about it. "Goddammit," he ranted to an intermediary. "Don't you know what I offered him? Why the f— didn't he take it?

After what the Bush people did to him . . ." Kerry was mystified. The Kerry camp made a last stab at persuading McCain
through actor Warren Beatty, an old friend of Shrum's and a
longtime Democratic activist. But McCain wasn't buying.
(After the election, a source close to Kerry said that it was an
adviser to McCain who first suggested that McCain might
wish to serve on the ticket with Kerry, but that the talks
were superficial and the idea was never thoroughly vetted.)

By then, Karl Rove had awakened to the threat of losing
McCain, and had begun to reel him back into the GOP tent.
In May, Rove met with McCain's adviser, John Weaver, at the
Caribou Coffee Shop down the block from the White
House. Rove and Weaver had once worked together on
Texas political campaigns before falling out (over money, it
was rumored; Rove reportedly spread smears about Weaver,
aggravating the wound). But now the two old hands made
peace and began planning for McCain's re-emergence as a
Republican stalwart. At a campaign event in Reno, Nev., on
June 18, the two old foes embraced. The sight of McCain's
hugging the president, or awkwardly trying to with his
POW-damaged arms, was so surprising that pundits assumed a quid pro quo. There wasn't any; McCain believed
that Bush was a more decisive war president, and he wanted
to keep his own party credentials burnished for a possible
presidential run in 2008.

With McCain a nonstarter, John Edwards was waiting—
and maneuvering and scheming—on the sidelines. Hours after bowing out of the presidential nomination race on
March 3, the senator from North Carolina had convened a

small circle of his closest advisers at his house on P Street in Georgetown. He wanted the vice presidential nomination, Edwards told his aides, he wanted it badly, and from that moment on was going to wage "a full-fledged campaign" to ensure that he got it. He knew there were risks; he knew the rules, he told his aides: you had to feign indifference, act as if running for veep had never crossed your mind. Edwards had heard the rumors that Kerry found him overly aggressive and ambitious. (The rumors were true. "What makes this guy think he can be president?" Kerry had whined to his staff when Edwards refused to give up all through February.) Edwards could end up pushing Kerry away. But he was convinced that his best, only hope was to make Kerry think he had no other choice.

Edwards was everywhere that spring campaigning for Kerry, especially in the closely contested border states. Edwards personally sought out every Kerry friend and adviser he could find, even venturing into New York City, where Southern accents don't always sell well. He appeared at a Goldman Sachs hedge-fund conference, hinting none too subtly to Big Business that the Millworker's Son could be their friend.

(The Bush camp watched the Edwards courtship with some skepticism. Rove, ever the organization man, figured that Gephardt would get the nod. Gephardt was Big Labor's man, and Kerry needed every union organizer he could find in swing states like Ohio and Pennsylvania. But pollster Dowd bet on Edwards: he believed that momentum would beat organization every time.)

In his usual solitary fashion, Kerry kept his decision close, not even telling his daughters, Alex and Vanessa, until the last second. ("I didn't want it to leak. I wanted to prove we could keep a secret," said Kerry.) The announcement, on July 6, was unusually early, timed to give the Kerry campaign a badly needed boost on the way to the convention in Boston at the end of the month. As it turned out, Kerry and Edwards got on right away, thanks to the universal male language. Both men were sports nuts (football and basketball for Edwards, windsurfing for Kerry, but jocks nonetheless). Their families were handsome and vigorous together. Only Teresa, with her unerring ability to call attention to herself, spoiled the picture. Viewing an otherwise golden-glow front-page *New York Times* photo, a reader's eye was drawn away from the toothy confidence of the candidates to Teresa's long arm reaching out to stop Edwards's youngest son, Jack, from sucking his thumb.

Behind the scenes, the McCain-for-veep gambit was not the only hot idea to flare up—then fizzle out—as the Kerry campaign groped for a bold stroke before the July convention. Kerry's aides were worried about the impact of the timing of the two conventions on the Democrats' campaign war chest. Under campaign-finance laws, each party's candidate was limited to spending $75 million in federal money between the nominating convention and the election in November. But since the Republicans would not convene until late August, the Democrats would have to stretch out their $75 million over a longer period—three months instead of two. In early March, the Kerry campaign began secretly debating a ploy: to put off formally accepting the Democratic nomination until September. The plan was to float the idea to a columnist (conservative Bob Novak, an old friend of Shrum's) and build up some momentum. On the first or second night of the convention, a delegate would dramatically and "spontaneously" rise up before the cameras and propose that Kerry delay his acceptance. The idea would take off like wildfire, leaving the candidate no choice but to accept the will of the party.

In mid-May, the idea leaked and was promptly ridiculed. Typical flip-flopping Kerry, jeered the Republicans: he'll attend the convention but he won't accept the nomination. The gimmick was quietly ditched. But another clever idea to beat the money game was just as quickly reborn, and it led to a fractious, exhausting and ultimately pointless struggle within the top command of the Kerry campaign.

Mary Beth Cahill, the campaign's stern boss, thought she had persuaded the candidate to forget about the radical suggestion of abandoning the federal spending limits altogether and trying to raise more than $75 million in private money after the convention. "Opting out" of the federal caps had saved the day for Kerry during the primaries, but Cahill worried that in the general election the Republicans would quickly follow suit—and, with the GOP's ability to raise money from big donors, swamp the Democrats. Cahill instructed her staff not to even mention the idea.

But Kerry, who had originally accepted Cahill's judgment, wavered. Cahill strongly suspected that Shrum had been whispering in his ear. She was furious: to her this was a battle not just between rival cliques but between haves and have-nots. The regular campaign staff, all on salary, wanted to do the prudent thing and stay within the public-finance system. But the media consultants—Shrum and his crowd—were paid a percentage of the money the campaign spent on ad buys. The more money for the campaign, Cahill knew, the more money for the consultants. Cahill was well aware of Shrum's reputation for running up the tab by buying ads whether his clients needed them or not. When Shrum was partnered with David Doak, their firm, Doak and Shrum, had been known as Soak and Run, and not just by competitors. But Cahill was careful not to cross Shrum personally. At a meeting of top staffers in early August, she bit her tongue: the senator wanted to hear a debate of the pros and cons. (After the election, Kerry said, "I did not waver. I was never presented with the facts. I wanted to have a careful vetting.")

Shrum lay low, avoiding personal confrontation (as usual, he had his own back channel). His more blunt partner, Tad Devine, made the pitch, reminding the group how the Democrats, short of money, had been forced to stop spending in Ohio in 2000, sacrificing a swing state they ended up losing by only 4 percentage points. "We were there with Al Gore in 2000 when he had to make the awful choice between Ohio and Florida," Devine said. "We'd hate to see you have to make that decision this time, Senator." Devine also assured the group that personal gain was not an issue—the consultants agreed to cap their fees and not profit from any additional spending on ads.

Kerry seemed impatient, distracted, even a little irritated. "Is José here?" he asked. "Where's José?" Everyone looked around, bewildered. Who was José? "Teresa's nephew, José," said Kerry. "Somebody go find José." The nephew, José Ferreira, was a Harvard M.B.A. whom Kerry relied upon for advice on strategy and communications. He was duly summoned, introduced by Kerry as a "math whiz" and told to make the argument he had made to Kerry and Teresa one night. A lengthy and inscrutable discussion of mathematical probabilities ensued. Campaign staffers looked around uneasily, but no one was willing to challenge Teresa's favorite nephew, a household fixture sometimes known as "the fourth son."

The old Kerry was back, the dithering candidate of the summer and fall of 2003 who had allowed meetings to go around in endless circles, arguing hypotheticals. He couldn't decide; he wanted more discussion, more numbers, more hurry up, then wait. The campaign's upper echelon seemed consumed by the opt-out question in June. Finally, John Sasso, a respected old Democratic hand who had run the Dukakis campaign in 1988, broke the deadlock. "Senator," said Sasso, "in my gut, this just doesn't feel right. You shouldn't be the first candidate to ever opt out of the public-finance system."

By now Cahill and her people were mildly panicking. If Kerry did decide to opt out, they would need to launch a major fund-raising campaign, and no plans had been made. So it was with relief, but also a sense of weariness, that Cahill finally told her staff, just days before the convention, that Kerry had decided he would stick with public financing.

Perhaps it's no wonder that the campaign, riven by feuds and fruitless argument, was unable to come up with a convincing theme or message. The message was the man: Kerry, the war hero, was the theme of the Democratic convention partly by default. There was to be no Bush-bashing, Bob Shrum decreed. Kerry, partly playing his old role of Devil's advocate to stir debate, had challenged Shrum. Why not attack the president? "Why not go after him?" Kerry asked. But Shrum had been talking to his father, a retired blue-collar worker who watched a lot of cable TV, and he had decided that voters were turned off by mudslinging. The campaign issued an edict: all convention speeches had to be cleared by the campaign before-hand. Any snarky lines were automatically cut out. (Only Al Sharpton ignored the rules and spoke hotly and twice as long as allotted.)

Kerry labored over his own speech, writing it out in long-hand. He had some famous help: input from legendary Kennedy family speechwriters Ted Sorensen and Richard Goodwin. Shrum worked with Kerry as well, flying commercial to meet Kerry secretly in hotel rooms on the campaign trail (to avoid stories that Shrum, the great wordsmith, was ghosting Kerry's speech). Kerry doggedly worked with media coach Michael Sheehan to speak more conversationally, more quickly, less deliberately, less pompously. The coaching, by and large, worked. "I'm John Kerry, and I'm reporting for duty," he began. The line brought down the house. It was originally meant to be the closing line in Sen. Max Cleland's speech introducing Kerry ("Tonight, Senator John Kerry is reporting for duty"), but the campaign decided it would work better as Kerry's opener. (Kerry's original opening line, "I'm John Kerry and I approve this message," a play on the disclaimer required of all political ads, was deemed too gimmicky and "insidery.")

Kerry had been standing tall as Highly Decorated Naval Officer all week. He "arrived" in Boston by boat, conjuring up images (it was hoped) of the brave Swift Boat commander (and ringing old echoes of JFK, the PT boat commander, and the patriot War of 1812 sailors of Old Ironsides, still moored in Boston Harbor). The stage at the convention hall was vaguely nautical, with its dark-wood podium and shipshape lines. Kerry's band of brothers, his Swift Boat crew, clambered onstage to stand with their old captain. The Democrats, never known for military precision, even managed to stay on time through the four evenings. Bill Clinton, a great orator as ever (overlooking his 1988 convention speech), pleased the faithful on the opening Monday night, but he (and any whiff of his draft-avoiding past) was long gone by the time Kerry and his gallant crew showed up.

By Thursday night, the Democrats were euphoric. Not all of their problems had gone away: Ralph Nader continued his independent candidacy, despite pleas from Democratic bigwigs. Still, the Democrats were feeling unusually unified.

Kerry's war record would help convince voters that he had what it took to be a commander in chief. Having such a hero on the top of the ticket would dispel those notions that Democrats are somehow soft, the "mommy party" to the Republicans' "daddy party."

One old warrior, however, had his doubts. Adm. William Crowe, former chairman of the Joint Chiefs of Staff, was among the phalanx of vets and top brass brought onstage as a kind of martial backdrop. He thought that the Democrats had gone overboard. Bringing up Vietnam was fine, he thought. Even stressing it. "But," he confided to a *Newsweek* reporter, "they pretty well drove it into the ground."

Are we there yet?: Kerry's bus-and-train trip gave the press plenty to dish about, starting with Teresa (Photo by Nick Danziger/Contact for *Newsweek*)

FIVE

On the Road:
All in the Family

There were strains and stumbles in the Kerry camp,
and the president's daughters took the stage
at the convention in New York.

L OOKING BACK, as Kerry staggered in late summer
and early fall, some Democrats wondered if July 29
would be remembered as the last truly happy night
of the campaign. It was the last night of the Democratic
convention, and the Kerry-Heinz house on Beacon Hill was
noisy and aglow. When the nominee walked through his
front door shortly after midnight, he was enveloped in a gust
of revelry. His guests, intoxicated by the moment and
Teresa's fine wines and champagnes, lavished praise on
Kerry's speech. Grinning, buoyant, the candidate kept apologizing for having raced through the applause lines. "I just
had to get it done in time," he kept saying. He had not
wanted to run over the witching hour of 11 P.M., when the

networks had threatened to cut him off to return to their regular programming.

Kerry's extended family, generations of WASPy-looking Forbes and Winthrop scions (Kerry had 32 first cousins on his mother's side), had marched up Beacon Hill to attend the party in force. Later, repairing to one of their ancestral haunts on Boston's North Shore, they observed how relaxed and gracious Teresa seemed to be that evening. A few years before, at her first family Thanksgiving with her proper Bostonian in-laws, Teresa had seemed to recoil at the Puritan simplicity of the affair. Kerry's cousins wondered if their shabby gentility failed to measure up to the lavish standards of the Pittsburgh heiress. But this night, in their grand house on Louisburg Square, as the waiters bustled about with heaping silver trays, she was in her element. To one of the Kerry cousins it really did seem like Camelot redux, a brief and shining moment—all too brief, as it turned out.

The Kerry for President "Sea to Shining Sea" tour left at 7 that morning, its participants hung over and exhausted. The 3,500-mile bus-and-train campaign tour was not a happy trip, certainly not for the candidate's wife. With each passing day she made less effort to hide her displeasure. Audiences were mystified when Teresa turned her back to them at daylight rallies and wore dark sunglasses and a hat at night (backstage, the candidate's wife complained of migraines and sore eyes). In town after town, state after state, she would flit about the stage, leaning in to make requests of her husband, sending him off on small errands—to fetch bottled water or deliver a message to an aide behind the scenes—while other people spoke. When she took the podium, audiences seemed baffled, and some cringed. Speaking of everything from clothes to her dead sister, she seemed to have a singular ability (though matched at times by her husband's) for sobering and silencing a cheering crowd.

The climax of the tour was an hourlong "family vacation" hike in the Grand Canyon. The idea was to watch Kerry's photogenic family appearing hale and vigorous on the way to a picturesque overlook, where Kerry would hold a press conference to castigate President Bush's environmental record. The imagery was not subtle: the Kerry family loves nature; Bush wants to ruin it.

VANESSA KERRY thought the whole thing was a little silly. Kerry's daughter, like her older sister, Alexandra, had appeared lovely and poised during their brief convention turn at the podium. But while Alex, an aspiring filmmaker and actress, seemed to enjoy playing the part of candidate's daughter, Vanessa was still having trouble saying goodbye to her private life. She traveled under an assumed name and, in the early days of the campaign, sometimes ran from well-wishers at airports. She had dropped out of Harvard Medical School for the year, partly to avoid the stares of her own teachers. Moving from her apartment in late June, she had been accosted by a man who said, "Hey, you look just like that Kerry girl." Lugging a bureau, dressed in a stained T-shirt, Vanessa replied, "You know, I get that all the time." "Don't worry about it," said the stranger. "She's not *that* bad-looking." (Kerry told the story to her father. When he got over laughing, he teased her mercilessly, repeating whenever she was cranky or sulky: "Don't worry about it, you're not *that* bad-looking.")

Now, as she hurried along a hiking path down the Grand Canyon, trying to get ahead of the press gaggle and enjoy the scenery without feeling like a TV prop, campaign handlers kept whispering, "You should hang back, walk with the family." Vanessa was unhappily muttering to herself about the absurdity of staged family vacations, but the reporters weren't noticing. They were too busy watching Teresa.

On the campaign bus, there had been constant talk of marital spats between the candidate and his wife for the past several days: Teresa wasn't speaking to her husband, she wanted to go home, she was driving the Secret Service crazy with her chronic lateness. Or so it appeared to the traveling press corps and not a few of Kerry's own entourage. The reporters and most of Kerry's staff did not realize that she was emotionally distraught over the recent death and illness of people close to her—an old and much-loved faithful retainer, a longtime family employee, had died the Saturday night before the convention, ten minutes before Teresa reached his bedside, and two nights later a sister-in-law was diagnosed with ovarian cancer. Teresa was also upset, Kerry later told *Newsweek*, because, at the convention, Kerry's handlers had decreed that Kerry and Edwards stand alone on stage for a long time taking in the applause. Teresa had urged that the candidates be quickly joined by their spouses and children to present a tableau of family unity.

That morning at the Grand Canyon, the press corps was atwitter over the rumor published in the Drudge Report that the night before in Flagstaff, Ariz., Teresa had requested separate accommodations from Kerry, on the other side of the Little America Hotel. ("It's wrong, they did not have separate rooms," said Kerry aide Michael Meehan.) On the Grand Canyon hike, Teresa was soon complaining of migraines and telling her husband she couldn't walk anymore. (Kerry says he frightened his wife by teasingly daring her to look over the edge. Afraid of heights, she seemed to push away from him.)

The happy-family-vacation scenario was disintegrating in plain view. The candidate tried to bravely soldier on, pulling along his sullen wife and children to show them the magnificent condors flying overhead. It was a losing battle; he was the only one who looked interested.

If Kerry felt stressed, he tried hard not to show it, but when he stepped in front of the microphones at the end of the trail, he fell flat on his face. A reporter did not want to ask the Democratic nominee about Bush's environmental record. He asked instead about a challenge the president had laid down a few days before. If Kerry had to do it all over again, knowing what he knew now, would he still have voted in support of the Iraq war?

"Yes," Kerry responded, then lapsed into Senate speak: "I would have voted for the authority. I believe it was the right authority for the president to have."

Kerry showed no recognition that he had just blundered. (Rule one of campaigning is to never answer a question posed by your opponent.) He spent a pleasant afternoon sitting in the back of the train talking to Vanessa about the meaning of life, challenging his daughter to think more deeply about life's eternal questions. At the other end of the train, in the crowded press car, reporters were struggling to make sense of what the candidate had said, or meant to say. Though they groused about the campaign's tardiness and loved to gossip about Teresa, the reporters on the Kerry tour were at the same time somewhat protective of the candidate and reluctant to pass on rumors. Kerry might not be the warmest or jolliest politician, but he was still their candidate, the man they spent day and night following around the country, and whom some of them might follow right to the most prestigious beat in Washington, the White House. Little hint of Teresa's demonstrative unhappiness crept into their stories, and the reporters sometimes gave the candidate the benefit of the doubt when he rambled or talked in circles. Reporters on a campaign plane are usually not competitive loners; over the days and weeks, they bond and at deadline time compare notes, out of a sense of collegiality and mutual self-defense.

At first, the general consensus among the boys and girls on the bus that day was that Kerry's remarks had been too indecipherable to constitute real news. Yes, Senator Kerry had said he would have voted for giving the president the "authority" to go to war, but was that really the same as approving of the decision to go to war? But as East Coast deadlines approached, the editors on the national desks of the big dailies—*The New York Times, The Washington Post, The*

Boston Globe—pressed: if the reporters wanted to make page one, they had to decide if this was really breaking news.

Competition, the pressure of time and possibly a weariness with Kerry's tiresome fondness for nuance and complexity pushed the reporters off the fence. Two days before, one of Kerry's foreign-policy advisers, Jamie Rubin, a top aide to former secretary of State Madeleine Albright, had told the *Post*'s Jim VandeHei that Kerry would have voted for the war "in all probability" even if no WMD had been found. Rubin later bitterly complained that he had been misquoted—he had added the stipulation that Kerry would have backed the war only with the support of many other nations and if Saddam had failed to comply with U.N. weapons inspectors. But the way the *Post* played the story— that Kerry did not regret his vote—helped push other editors at other papers to take the same line. As the story was played the next day in the big papers, then in all the media outlets, Kerry was signaling that he was in essential agreement with the president's decision to go to war. (Kerry later said that he had wanted Rubin to go out and correct the record right away. "It didn't happen," he said. "Mistakes were made.")

After trudging along after the Kerry family vacation and sparring with their editors, the reporters were testy and ornery. Though they kept Teresa's sometimes erratic behavior out of their copy, when they were speaking among themselves, in the privacy of the campaign "bubble," the reporters were increasingly vocal about mocking the candidate's wife. Like Nancy Reagan before her, Teresa was a tempting target for jaded reporters. When the train rolled into Kingman, Ariz., its final stop, late that evening, the print scribes and TV crews collectively groaned at the sight of a large crowd gathered to greet the senator and his family at the train. One wise guy from the Fourth Estate wondered aloud, in fairly blunt language, whether the campaign could cancel a late-night rally on the grounds that Teresa was indisposed. The reporters guffawed and joked about Teresa-as-diva for the rest of the cross-country tour.

At Bush-Cheney headquarters in Arlington, Va., they were watching and wondering—and gloating and snickering. The BC04 operatives could only guess at any strains in the Kerry-Heinz family (though they tried, closely monitoring the Drudge Report, which broadcast some of the rumors). But Kerry's stumbling was plain to see. In mid-August, Steve Schmidt, the bullet-headed boss of the Bush-Cheney campaign "rapid response," sat in the reflected glow of TV sets, beneath the skull of a cow, lecturing a pair of *Newsweek* reporters on the ineptitude of the Kerry campaign. On a whiteboard behind his desk he sketched out a grid with a Magic Marker, dividing the upper-left quadrant into smaller and smaller sections. "Every time he has put forward a new position [on Iraq]," Schmidt explained, "he's narrowed the field. Here's where he is now: he's in a small corner." On its Web site the Republican National Committee had posted a 14-minute "documentary" that laid out Kerry's ever more thinly sliced explanations for his Iraq votes. Kerry was slowly tying his own feet together. From time to time, the Bush-Cheney campaign would give him a little shove.

THE BUSHIES ALMOST SEEMED to feel sorry for the Kerry campaign, in a condescending sort of way. Under constant scrutiny, all candidates misstep during the course of a long campaign. At his April press conference, Bush, frozen in front of the cameras, had been unable to think of a single mistake he had made since 9/11. In August the president told a reporter that the war on terror was unwinnable and had to hastily "clarify" his remarks. In his familiar role of Dr. Doom, the designated hit man, Vice President Cheney suggested, outrageously, that by voting for Kerry Americans could be inviting another terrorist attack. Yet Bush and Cheney seemed to waltz away from their clumsy or embarrassing moments. Kerry, on the other hand, just dug himself into deeper holes. Somehow the Bush-Cheney campaign was able to keep Kerry's mistakes in the news, while the Kerry campaign was unable to do likewise with Bush's blunders.

BC04 operatives mocked the bumbling of their opponents while crediting their own genius. Schmidt was quietly contemptuous and cocky. At the Democratic convention he established himself in a frontline war room in a small building near the convention hall. Pacing and glowering and barking into his phone, Schmidt watched a pair of TV sets looking for something to ridicule. At one point in his speech Kerry asked, "What does it mean when 25 percent of the children in Harlem have asthma because of air pollution?" But he mispronounced "air"; it sounded as if the senator had said "hair pollution" instead. The Bushies, who loved to deride Kerry as an effete Frenchman and Edwards as a pretty boy, found this hilarious. "Hair pollution?" Schmidt asked, laughing. "He *has* nice hair," remarked Tim Griffin, the RNC's head of opposition research. (The Bushies liked to make fun of Kerry's tastes. When the Democratic candidate went to a Kansas City, Mo., barbecue joint, Kerry, who had once ordered Swiss cheese on a Philadelphia cheese steak, picked unenthusiastically at the greasy ribs before retiring to his campaign plane, presumably to dine on asparagus tips. The BC04 staff was so amused by this story, and so eager to celebrate their own regular-guy manliness, that they had the rib joint cater a meal for reporters on Air Force One.)

The Kerry campaign seemed trumped by some of the oldest tricks. Matthew Dowd, the pollster and chief of the BC04 "Strategery Department," kept predicting to reporters that if history was an indicator, Kerry would get a 15-point bounce out of the Democratic convention. The prediction, though inflated and intended to create false expectations, was widely played in the press. Kerry came out of Boston with little or no boost in the polls. (Adman Mark McKinnon laughed about a "dead-cat bounce," from a sick Wall Street joke: even a dead cat bounces if dropped from a high enough ledge.) Dowd then set about lowering expectations for Bush, saying that, historically, the incumbent gets only about two-thirds of the challenger's postconvention bounce. Since two-thirds of zero is zero, that's about what Bush would get, Dowd insisted to reporters. The whole exercise was a transparent effort to spin, to play the old expectations game. The average bounce for an incumbent was more like 10 percent. "But they [the Kerry campaign] never said it!"

raved McKinnon. "Ever! They could have at least pushed back!"

The Kerry campaign made much more fundamental mistakes, at least in the view of the Bush-Cheney team. Kerry and his advisers failed to understand that the election would not be decided by the candidates' stands on the issues, but rather by more visceral concerns. Dowd and Karl Rove were wonkish students of academic literature on voter attitudes, lapping up obscure studies on such matters as turnout and target precincts. But they didn't need to read much to understand that post–9/11 voters cared more about strength and resolve than a candidate's 10-point plan to reform immigration or Medicare. Kerry bounced around from issue to issue, theme to theme, while Bush stuck with one overriding message: unwavering strength. ("Wrong and strong," the pundits began to write, "beats bright and right.")

GEORGE W. BUSH HAS NO USE for psychobabble about his persona. "If you're the president, you don't have time to try to figure out who you are," he told a pair of *Newsweek* reporters aboard Air Force One in August. "I think it's unfair to the American people to sit in that Oval Office and try to find your inner soul." But that didn't stop his aides from trying to define the inner Bush for voters. In August, McKinnon gathered his media team for a brunch at Oscar's in Manhattan's Waldorf-Astoria to talk about polls but also to listen to a psychoanalyst named Stanley Renshon. The author of a mostly sympathetic book on the Bush family called

In His Father's Shadow, Renshon argued that voters wanted a president who could be both a strong leader and a consensus maker, two qualities that did not always go together. After 9/11, Americans wanted a hero—someone who would "mount the ramparts and charge up the hill," as Renshon put it—but they still wanted the president to be a warm, reassuring Everyman. As they asked questions at the restaurant that day, Bush's team wanted to know: how do you bridge the gap between the two?

The president needed someone who could bring out his softer, warmer side. So it was with a sense of relief that the Bushies welcomed Karen Hughes back onto the president's plane in August. Despite her decision in the spring of 2002 to go home to Austin to be with her family, the former White House communications director had never vanished altogether—she worked on Bush's big speeches and often chatted with Laura about kids and decorating. But it was important to have her imposing yet soothing presence near Bush as he campaigned. She was able to tell the candidate what he didn't want to hear, to walk "into the propellers," as McKinnon put it, and she had a good ear for lines that would appeal to women and moderate swing voters.

To serve red meat at the convention the Bush campaign enlisted Arnold Schwarzenegger, the Hollywood Terminator who had successfully recast himself as the California "Governator." Campaign advisers were slightly uneasy about whether "Ah-nold" would come on too strong for the folks back home. But in his prime-time convention address, the BC04 apparatus let the Governator get off his signature line,

"Don't be economic girlie men!" (Afterward, Schwarzenegger called his speechwriter, Landon Parvin, from the convention hall. Parvin could hear the roaring crowd in the background. Schwarzenegger told the speechwriter he was glad the campaign hadn't nixed the "girlie man" line. "It just took the roof off the place," said Schwarzenegger.)

The convention planners also worried about overdoing 9/11. They had planned to introduce Bush by playing an emotional video for a Michael W. Smith song called "There She Stands," which played on the imagery of the Stars and Stripes over Ground Zero. When McKinnon first saw the video, he started to weep. But some staffers were concerned that the press would accuse the campaign of wrapping Bush in the flag. ("Too patriotic?" McKinnon asked himself. "And the problem with that would be?")

Peggy Noonan, Ronald Reagan's old speechwriter, was drafted to craft a script for a new video. She had writer's block. "I'm just not getting it, guys," she told the BC04 team. "It's just not there." The campaign sent Noonan a bunch of photos and told her to try harder. McKinnon tried to imagine the speechwriter—a "feeler," he called her, "she's very artistic, very poetic . . . she's a *feeler*"—using the photos to get over her block. He thought of Noonan "getting naked and rubbing the pictures, lighting incense, channeling." Whatever: it seemed to work. A few days before the speech, Noonan delivered her script. The president's appearance was preceded by a short, moving video and no introduction. Bush just walked out on the convention floor. The faithful went wild.

Kerry had sweated visibly through his acceptance speech. "He's sweating like Nixon!" Steve Schmidt had sneered from his war-room perch. For Bush's speech, Madison Square Garden was as cold as a meat locker. Shivering correspondents were delighted to receive printed copies of Bush's remarks, hot off the photocopier. "It's warm," said *USA Today*'s Judy Keen, sighing and holding the document to her icy cheek.

Bush had been a little disappointed that his own daughters did not seem to like politics. When he was 18 he had traveled around Texas with his father as the senior Bush ran for the U.S. Senate (he lost that 1964 race to Democrat Ralph Yarborough). George W. Bush had been emotionally involved in his father's campaigns, recalled Laura. But not the twins. The girls could have been involved with their father's presidential campaign in 2000, when they turned 18, but they chose not to, wishing to preserve their anonymity when they went off to college (the press did give them a zone of privacy, except when they were caught using fake IDs to drink alcohol). Jenna had begged her father not to run for president in 2000. "Oh, I just wish you wouldn't run," she had told him. "It's going to change our life." Bush had replied, "You know, Jenna, your mother and I are living our lives. And that's what we raised you and Barbara to do: live yours."

SOMETIME DURING THE WINTER OF 2003–04, her last at the University of Texas, Jenna Bush had a bad dream, according to her mother. In the dream she imagined her father losing the election. Jenna had a revelation. She wanted to be with her father and be involved in the campaign. She called her mother and sent her father a message telling him about her desire to help. "It was very moving to George," the First Lady told *Newsweek*.

The girls had always been a little naive about the press. During Barbara's time at Yale, a publication got wind of her summer internship in New York and was preparing to publish an item. "Can you call them up and tell them not to write that?" Barbara asked a White House press aide. The aide suppressed a sigh and explained reality. The twins had taken their lumps from time to time for their partying, but they were unprepared for the coverage of their attempt to be humorous at the convention. The speech had felt like a bad inside joke; grandmother Barbara Bush looked aghast when the twins tried to crack a joke about what "Gammy" thought of "Sex and the City." The twins simpered and giggled through it, but they were hurt by the reviews. "Lame," wrote a *New York Times* critic, and that was one of the kinder judgments. (The speech had been largely written by Karen Hughes. It was well known within the Bush campaign that humor was not Hughes's forte. The president teased her, "Karen, you're not the funny one.")

And yet the twins did not sulk, at least for long. They went back out on the campaign trail with their father and had fun. The girls had been on the bus off and on through August. The president clearly enjoyed having them along for the ride; the former fraternity-rush chairman chuckled as his daughters called out derisive signs they saw along the road.

Passing a YOU SUCK! father and daughters howled with sophomoric glee.

The girls, especially Jenna, had more than a touch of their father's in-your-face showmanship. Jenna got the hang of working an audience. At the University of Wisconsin, Oshkosh, she paused at what was clearly meant to be an applause line in her speech. When no one clapped, she looked straight at a girl in the front row and said, "Clap!" As the audience dutifully clapped, Jenna turned to Barbara and both girls laughed. Boys kept approaching the girls insisting, "My mom really wants me to take a picture with you two." By the third time around, Jenna simply replied, "Ohhh, really?" As they left an event in Milwaukee, hecklers held up a sign saying SEND THE BUSH TWINS TO IRAQ. A male student yelled out, "No way, don't send them to Iraq. Send them to my room!"

The twins were beginning to enjoy the dynastic imperative. At the wedding of their cousin George P. Bush at the family compound in Kennebunkport, Me., in August, Jenna and some other cousins stood to propose a toast. They raised a glass to George P. and his future bride—the president and First Lady, "2024 or something," Laura Bush recalled to *Newsweek*.

Laura has a wistful quality about her. She had been observing the Bush family for many years, and she could tell how they had been forever changed by their proximity to power. She did not daydream about going back to the ranch. "I guess in some ways there's an idea of relief at the end, whenever that is . . . ." But she went on, "Your life isn't ever the same—it isn't like you go back to a life that you had before. I mean, we might go back to our home, but your life is always so different after having been here [at the White House]. And so I think you're aware of that the whole time . . . You'll never be anonymous again. It'll be a different life."

The First Lady was a benign presence in the campaign. She was amused by the omnipotent Rove. "I love Karl," she told a *Newsweek* reporter. "He's fun to be with. He reminds me of Pigpen [the "Peanuts" character who walks around in a cloud of dirt]. Like ideas come off of him, the dirt . . . you know how his hair kind of all stands up at the top." She thought Rove got too much credit and too much blame. "I love to call him for the scoop," she said. "I love to gossip with him. And hear what he has to allow."

Bush's convention was regarded as a success, a classic exercise in Republican message discipline. The president seemed to get a good if temporary bounce, as much as 10 points measured by some polls. But the real movement in the campaign was happening offstage, in the netherworld occupied by the so-called 527s.

Named after the provision of the tax code that sets the rules for political-advocacy groups, the 527s had become the latest proof of an eternal truth: "Money always finds a way." The truism was uttered, somewhat resignedly, by John McCain, the coauthor of the latest attempt to control the flow of money into politics, the 2002 McCain-Feingold bill. The other essential truth for campaign-finance reformers is the immutable Law of Unintended Consequences. The great achievement of McCain-Feingold was to outlaw soft money—limitless donations flowing to the political parties (the result of a loophole carved in the 1980s to get around the limits on individual contributions to candidates). But no sooner had the ink dried on McCain-Feingold than the big donors began writing their checks to independent advocacy groups—the so-called 527s—so they could support one or another candidate. New, heavily financed groups, like MoveOn.org, popped up to push their agendas. With lax disclosure requirements, it was not always easy to tell who was pulling the strings behind these groups.

The Democrats, traditionally lagging behind the wealthier and more corporate Republicans at political fund-raising, were quick to jump on the 527s as a great equalizer. When Kerry was essentially broke in March, it was the 527s that poured money into ads bashing Bush, partially offsetting the Bush campaign's very effective "flip-flop" ads.

By law, the candidates and the political parties were not supposed to coordinate with the 527s. But that didn't stop the 527s from coordinating with each other. Ground zero of the Democrats' 527 explosion was a nondescript suite in a building two blocks from the White House. This was the office of the Thunder Road Group, the consulting firm run by Jim Jordan—who, until he was fired in November, had been Kerry's campaign manager. Jordan was careful not to talk directly to his old comrades at the Kerry campaign, but he didn't need to. He could be very useful in helping to run a new get-out-the-vote operation called America Coming Together. ACT was busily registering record numbers of voters in Democratic strongholds, especially new voters in black and poor areas. When ACT registered a new voter, it passed on key information about the voter's interest to another 527 housed in Jordan's office called America Votes. This was an umbrella operation, coordinating between dozens of advocacy groups, from environmentalists to abortion-rights activists to gun-control crusaders. Armed with the data from ACT, these groups could target the new voters with direct mail. A third 527, the Media Fund, ran TV ads attacking Bush. It was at once a cozy and vast operation. By June the three 527s sharing office space at the Thunder Road Group had spent $60 million to elect John Kerry.

The Democratic 527s were well funded and influential. Indeed, the Democrats were counting on them to boost voter turnout in key swing states—to make the difference for Kerry in November. But in August, by far the most powerful 527 was neither Democratic nor very rich. It was called Swift Boat Veterans for Truth.

BEN GINSBERG WAS THE CHIEF LAWYER for the Bush-Cheney 2004 campaign. But he handled other clients as well, and in July he was approached by a group of Vietnam veterans who wanted some legal advice. They were angry, they said, about historian Douglas Brinkley's Vietnam War biography of Kerry, *Tour of Duty*. They said they had served in Swift Boats with Kerry, and that he had exaggerated or even lied about his exploits, while denigrating his old buddies as war criminals. Because of his three Purple Hearts (one undeserved, according to the Swifties), Kerry had been allowed to go home to preen for the cameras, while the rest of them were stuck in the Mekong Delta. Still nursing the resentments of more than three decades, the Swift Boat vets were raising money to run an ad exposing Kerry. They needed a lawyer to help them navigate the campaign-finance laws.

Ginsberg liked the vets. He had been feeling guilty about his generation's sneering contempt for the military as a Vietnam-era college student. He wanted to help out. He did not worry—at the time—that it would be somehow improper for the Bush-Cheney campaign lawyer to be advising a 527 group. He wasn't doing anything that the other side wasn't already doing, he figured. He knew that the lawyers in the Kerry campaign and at the DNC were giving legal counsel to 527s, and nobody seemed to object. Besides, the Swift Boat vets didn't think they'd cause much of a stir. At a picnic on a muggy night in July, they told Ginsberg that they were pretty sure the establishment press would just blow them off.

LATER, AFTER THE SWIFT BOAT ADS became a sensation that threatened to sink the Kerry campaign, not a few pundits and politicos speculated that Karl Rove had been behind the whole thing. After all, Rove was reputed to be a great lover of political dirty tricks, an expert at running smear campaigns through go-betweens or, in spy jargon, "cutouts." Rove was an old friend of a wealthy Texan named Bob Perry, who had given the Swift Boat vets $200,000 to buy some ads. Rove insisted that he had not spoken to Perry in more than a year and that he had played no role in setting up the Swift Boat vets, but political insiders all winked knowingly at each other.

Rove is a likely and even plausible target for conspiracy theories. But if he was running a covert operation to attack Kerry through the Swift Boat vets, it was a pretty sloppy one. How could he have allowed BC04's own lawyer to represent the vets if he wanted to conceal the hand of the Bush campaign? Ginsberg maintains that he never told Rove he had taken on the Swifties as clients; even so, if Rove had been worried about disguising any link between the Bush campaign and the Swift Boat vets, he would presumably have taken more pains to warn top BC04 staffers to keep their hands off.

Ginsberg realized soon enough that he had an image problem working for the Swift Boat vets at the same time that he was representing BC04. A few days before the Republican convention, he was called by Jim Rutenberg of *The New York Times*. Rutenberg had been tipped off to Ginsberg's role, presumably by the Democrats. At first Ginsberg tried to argue with the *Times* reporter that there was nothing improper, no story here, but he had a sinking feeling that he would soon be reading about himself in the papers. He called Rove and the other top BC04 officials and offered to resign from the campaign. They told him to hold off until they saw Rutenberg's article in print.

At about 11 P.M., a very agitated Ginsberg was waiting to read the early online version of the next day's *New York Times* when Rutenberg called. "God, we just thought of something," said Rutenberg (as Ginsberg recalled the conversation). "This isn't going to have any impact on your role in the campaign, is it? We haven't, like, screwed you over?" Ginsberg responded, "You've got to be kidding me. How f—ing out to lunch are you!" (Rutenberg agreed his conversations with Ginsberg were heated, but said he was misquoted—that he never said, "We haven't, like, screwed you over?"—and insisted to *Newsweek* that the *Times* was fair in its reporting on both Republican and Democratic 527s.) Before Ginsberg could hurl the phone against the wall, he hung up. He wrote his letter of resignation at 4 A.M. As he watched the story of his demise that morning on CNN, he noticed old photos of him from the 2000 campaign. He was taken aback at how much grayer his hair had become.

SIX

New Battles: The Vets Attack

Underestimating the Swift Boat ads,
the Kerry team suffered from their slow response.
Then Bill Clinton's former aides arrived
and staged a silent coup.

THE ATTACK OF the Swift Boat vets did not catch the Kerry campaign by surprise, not entirely at least. Kerry's operatives had worried from the beginning that some right-wing group would try to use his old Vietnam antiwar speeches against him. In the summer of 2003 the Kerry campaign had quietly made some inquiries with C-Span, asking the cable network not to release old videotapes of Kerry as an angry young vet fulminating about war crimes and atrocities. Portions of his sometimes overwrought testimony before the Senate Foreign Relations Committee in 1971 could be twisted into an attack ad, the Kerryites feared. They were told not to worry: the rules prohibited the use of the tapes for political advertising. (When the Swift Boat vets made ads attacking Kerry with images from his 1971 testimony, they used an audio but not a video tape.)

In August, when the Swift Boat vets scheduled a press conference at the National Press Club, the Kerry campaign dispatched Gen. Wesley Clark to hold a counter–press conference. At the last minute the Swifties canceled. A cheer went up at Kerry-Edwards headquarters on 15th Street in Washington.

The cheers were premature. The Swift Boat ads—a first round charging that Kerry had lied to win his medals, then a second batch accusing him of betraying his mates by calling them war criminals—were misleading, but they were very effective. The Kerry high command failed to see the potential for damage until it was too late.

To respond to the ads would be to dignify them, argued both Bob Shrum and Mary Beth Cahill. Mostly the ads were stirring up the Republican true believers, not winning over the "persuadables," the undecided voters. At least that's what most of Kerry's advisers wanted to believe. It would be a mistake for him to hit back; the persuadables don't like negative campaigning. Better to float above it all.

But Kerry's pollster, Mark Mellman, wasn't so sure. He could see that the Swift Boat ads were having an impact— not much at the very beginning, but soon a measurable dent in Kerry's support. The old-fashioned mainstream press was ignoring the claims of the Swifties, but on Fox News, the "fair and balanced" cable network whose viewership was

Looking good: The president was surging in the polls

(Photo by Charles Ommanney/Contact for *Newsweek*)

rough 80 percent pro-Bush, the Swifties were getting plenty of air time. And not just on Fox. Other cable networks, possibly trying to catch up with their flag-waving (and higher-rated) competitor, had jumped into the fray. The Swifties had bought only a few hundred thousand dollars' worth of ads, but each played over and over—free—on the cable channels, CNN and MSNBC as well as Fox. The Swift Boat charges were the source of constant debate in the blogosphere, the new online world of bloggers, the modern-day Internet pamphleteers whose screeds were widely read—especially by the young bookers and producers who set the agenda on cable TV.

WITH ALL THIS CHURNING in the new media, the story was bound to spill out into the undecided electorate. Mellman could see it in the numbers. So, too, could Kerry's old campaign manager, Jim Jordan. As an adviser to America Coming Together, he saw lots of polling. He could see that in West Virginia, a key battleground state, 65 percent of voters told one survey that they had seen the group's first ad, which was impossible—but they had clearly heard about it. A fairly small slice—16 percent—said the ad made them feel less favorable to Kerry. Jordan knew that the real number was higher. People don't like to admit that they're influenced by propaganda.

Kerry himself was itching to hit back at the Swift Boat vets. He had been warned by a McCain aide two years earlier to watch out for the mudslingers on the Republican right. "They'll make it look like you fought for the Viet Cong," said the McCain aide, recalling the dirty tricks played on his own boss in the 2000 primaries. Kerry was furious at former senator Bob Dole, who had gone on TV to say that not all the Swift Boat veterans could be Republican liars. Kerry called his old Senate colleague (and fellow Purple Heart recipient). "You can't say this kind of stuff," Kerry lit into Dole, "and by the way, Bob, I bled from every one of my wounds." Dole blathered that Kerry was a great friend and that he admired him, but he didn't take back what he had said. ("He's an attack dog rehabbed as a statesman, and then he allows himself to be wheeled out for this," growled Shrum, in the midst of a fulmination about "the Big Lie.")

Kerry wanted to blister the Swift Boat vets in a speech he was scheduled to give to the Veterans of Foreign Wars on Aug. 18. "We need to get these guys," he said. But at the last minute his handlers on the road were ordered by headquarters in Washington to restrain the candidate. Cahill and Shrum were worried that Kerry would seem too bitter and angry, the way he had appeared when he sarcastically thanked "Good Morning Americas'" Charlie Gibson, back in April, for doing the Republicans' dirty work.

Kerry's running mate, John Edwards, also wanted to take a swipe at the Swifties. Edwards was hardly an attacker in the Dole (or Cheney) tradition of vice presidential hit men; his whole persona and appeal were based on sunny optimism. But as early as Aug. 5, when the Swifties were just getting traction, Edwards wanted to push back, hard. McCain had just told the Associated Press that the Swift Boat ads were "dishonest and dishonorable . . . the same kind of deal that was pulled on me." Edwards wanted to begin a speech, "I join with Senator McCain in calling on the president to condemn this dishonest and dishonorable ad." But Kerry headquarters said no. Stephanie Cutter, the boss of the Kerry communications shop, wanted to hit back, but Shrum and Cahill insisted that the campaign didn't need to give the Swift Boat vets any more attention than they were already getting.

Edwards played along, but his aides were indignant. They warned the veep candidate that the story was already out of control and about to get worse. Historian Douglas Brinkley cautioned that Kerry's diary included mention of a meeting with some North Vietnamese in Paris. Edwards was flabbergasted. "Let me get this straight," the senator said. "He met with terrorists? Oh, that's good."

Kerry was personally hurt by the Swift Boat attacks on his valor and honor. On his cell phone, he called Vanessa several times in August to vent about the Swift Boat vets. He would go on about the unfairness of it all. Vanessa could hear the anguish in his voice.

The pain reached deep into the Kerry family. His first wife, Julia Thorne, had been the forgotten woman of the campaign. Divorced from Kerry since 1988, she lived quietly in Montana, recovered from bouts of depression that had plagued her as the privately unhappy wife of a very public man. Thorne never gave interviews, but she was watching the campaign closely, talking to her daughters, Alexandra and Vanessa, at least once a day. She was very upset, she told

Vanessa. She could remember how Kerry had suffered in Vietnam; she had seen the scars on his body, heard him cry out in his nightmares. She was so agitated about the unfairness of the Swift Boat assault that she told Vanessa she was ready to break her silence, to speak out and personally answer the Swift Boat charges. She changed her mind only when she was reassured that the campaign was about to start fighting back hard.

But Kerry's old ambivalence and caution were surfacing once again. At home he had always been reticent about telling his daughters about the war. They were intensely curious, and they knew their father had suffered. But he would not tell them exactly how. They never knew he had killed someone until they read about it in the newspapers. Alex had become a professional filmmaker. Her first short film was the "fictional" tale of a daughter struggling to connect with her father, a shellshocked veteran of a war reminiscent of Vietnam.

Vanessa assumed that her father was not hitting back because he did not like the dirty side of politics. The Kerry girls saw their father as a pillar of New England rectitude. He had never punished them for being late or for petty rule breaking, only for failing to tell the truth. He would invoke their Brahmin ancestors, looking at them sternly and intoning, "Vanessa *Bradford* Kerry," "Alexandra *Forbes* Kerry."

The girls were frustrated. At campaign events, voters would come up to Vanessa and say, "Did your dad really deserve his medals?" Why couldn't her father set them straight? He wouldn't be lying; he'd be telling the truth.

Kerry wanted the truth to come out, but he wanted to get it out in his own careful, deliberate way. The former prosecutor wanted to marshal the evidence, to build a case that would hold up. But that took time, and in the world of bloggers and 24/7 talking heads on cable, every day spent fact checking was a day lost. One quick pre-emptive strike might have been to reassemble Kerry's old Swift Boat crew, his band of brothers, and send them out on the talk-show circuit. But it was August; they were mostly a bunch of grandfathers, scattered on family vacations. Kerry remembered that one of the Swift Boat commanders, Donald Droz, killed in Vietnam, had regularly written his wife. Maybe one of those letters detailed the battle in which Kerry had won a Bronze Star and his last Purple Heart (the Swift Boat Veterans for Truth were claiming that no shots had been fired). The campaign scrambled to find the wife, but she explained that she had no letters about the incident; she had seen her husband in Hawaii soon after on R&R, so there had been no need for letters. Kerry couldn't believe it. "Let me call her," he said. The whole process took four or five days, and the letters never turned up.

T HE KERRY CAMPAIGN did work closely with the major dailies, feeding documents to *The New York Times, The Washington Post* and *The Boston Globe* to debunk the Swift Boat vets. The articles were mostly (though not entirely) supportive of Kerry, but it was too late. The old media may have been more responsible than the new media, but they were also largely irrelevant.

In early August, when the Swift Boat story started to pick up steam on the talk shows, Susan Estrich, a California law professor, well-known liberal talking head and onetime campaign manager for Michael Dukakis, had called the Kerry campaign for marching orders. She had been booked on Fox's "Hannity & Colmes" to talk about the Swift Boat ads. What are the talking points? Estrich asked the Kerry campaign. There are none, she was told. Estrich was startled. She had seen this bad movie before. In August 1988, Dukakis had blown a 17-point lead over Vice President George H.W. Bush by failing to hit back against a series of seemingly petty or low-blow attacks (including allegations of mental instability). Sitting in a bar at New York's Essex House hotel, in town as a liberal TV commentator at the Republican convention, Estrich gloomily replayed the tape in her head. "Dukakis is not crazy; details at 11," she bitterly mimicked a TV announcer caught up in the swirl of the Bush I smear campaign of 1988. Kerry's August was just like Dukakis's August, she despaired. Even some of the people were the same, on both sides. Estrich e-mailed her friend Marylouise Oates, better known as Oatsie. Married to Bob Shrum, Oatsie was on Nantucket at the time with Kerry and the inner circle. "Do something," pleaded Estrich. She wouldn't reveal what Oatsie e-mailed back, but she said, "They know. They're shellshocked."

In mid-September CBS's "60 Minutes II" aired a sensational report, claiming to have obtained long-lost records of George W. Bush's superior officer in the Texas Air National Guard complaining that Bush had shirked his duty. For a moment it looked as if the tables had turned, and Bush would have to endure an uncomfortable round of questions about his spotty attendance record in the stateside guard while Kerry had been dodging bullets in the Mekong Delta. But the moment did not last. Even before the "60 Minutes" segment finished airing, a blogger was up on the Web questioning whether the documents were fakes. The story quickly turned from Bush's war record to Dan Rather's carelessness and overzealousness—and even to the question of whether CBS had been secretly working with the Democrats to smear Bush. Rather and CBS kept the story alive by refusing to admit error. The Democratic involvement in the story was minimal and essentially meaningless, but the whole flap diverted attention away from questions, never entirely resolved, about whether Bush had skipped out on his guard service.

At a Q&A session with reporters after the "60 Minutes" story broke, Laura Bush said that she doubted the authenticity of the documents. The White House had been lying low, not wanting to get dragged into the controversy. The cable-news pundits crowed over the brilliant strategy of having the First Lady attack the documents instead. At the White House, everyone had a good laugh. Laura's comments were off the cuff, not part of some clever West Wing strategy. Sometimes Karl Rove's well-disciplined message machine was just a mirage.

The men and women around the president were brimming with confidence and condescension toward the Kerry team.

Most of Bush's top political advisers had been with him since his days as governor of Texas. Rove and Hughes, McKinnon and Dowd had exulted and suffered through the wild ride of election night 2000. They saw themselves as a family, not without stresses and rivalries, but bonded by victory and adversity. They were intensely loyal to the president, who demanded absolute and unquestioning fealty. The Bushites looked on the Kerryites, by contrast, as a band of mercenaries working for a Captain Queeg. Kerry depended on hired guns because he was unable to command the affection and devotion of his subordinates, the Bush aides thought. They believed they were winning the election because they had the better candidate but also because they were better organized and just plain smarter than the opposition.

Bush was feeling jubilant as he plunged into the September crowds. Minnesota had been regarded as a swing state, but just barely. It had gone Democratic every election since 1976. As he pored over recent state polls that showed him surging ahead, the president was incredulous. "If we carry Minnesota," he said, "we win big." Bush seemed to be enjoying the discomfiture of Dan Rather and CBS over the phony documents. At a press conference in mid-September with interim Iraqi Prime Minister Ayad Allawi, Bush called out, "Is anybody here from CBS?" He sounded more needling than gracious.

His father had been worrying. The elder Bush's ulcers had been acting up. Bush senior had watched the "60 Minutes" "scoop" with rising indignation. He disliked the "60 Minutes II" anchorman, Dan Rather, who had staged a hostile confrontation with the then Vice President Bush in an interview during the 1988 campaign. George H.W. Bush was by and large an optimist and a forgiving man. But he nurtured long grudges against certain reporters, and Rather was one of them. Lately Bush senior had been keeping a sleeve of saltine crackers on his desk to tamp down his bile. He would munch on the crackers as he watched the talking heads and the evening news, his stomach churning.

But on Friday, Sept. 17, Gallup released a poll showing his son ahead of Kerry by an astonishing 13 points. Other polls showed the race closer, but Poppy was ecstatic. He fired off an e-mail to one of his aides. "Let's just say the e-mail had exclamation points," said the aide, laughing.

Kerry felt alone and isolated. It was not an unfamiliar feeling. His father had been a Foreign Service officer stationed in Berlin. As a boy, shipped off to a severe Swiss boarding school by his remote yet demanding father, Kerry had to take a night train through communist East Germany. The cold war had been at its coldest and darkest in Germany in the early 1950s. Recounting his memories to a *Newsweek* reporter in the summer of 2004, Kerry could vividly picture himself clutching a piece of paper with directions written out by his parents—a somber, long-faced boy, traveling alone across a forbidding landscape, fearful but determined not to show it.

When Kerry was alone and feeling the unfairness of things, he sometimes lashed out and blamed others. He would call his advisers at all hours of the night. On a Saturday evening in late August, Tad Devine, Bob Shrum's partner and fellow media man and strategic adviser, was studying for an appearance on "Meet the Press" the next morning when Kerry called him. Devine was weary and in no mood to talk to the candidate. Kerry offered to call back later. "The most important thing is that I get a good night's sleep," the blunt-spoken Devine told his client. "Don't call me." Kerry had been ostensibly phoning to offer advice, but he blurted out what was really on his mind: the attack of the Swift Boat veterans. "It's a pack of f—ing lies, what they're saying about me," he fairly shouted over the phone.

Kerry blamed his advisers for his predicament. He had wanted to fight back; they had counseled caution. His honor was being dragged through the mud, and now he was being mocked for not standing up for himself. He wanted to turn on someone. Not a few staffers and advisers in the badly frayed Kerry camp believed that the candidate should blame his well-paid media consultants. Surveying the damage in late summer, a Democratic strategist privately scorned the media consultants for the narrowness, if not the selfishness, of their vision. Shrum and Devine were in the advertising business, this strategist said. All they really understood was the air war. They put their faith in (and fattened their pocketbooks with) paid political ads. When the Kerry campaign opted not to abandon the campaign-finance system and instead to stick with its allotted $75 million in federal funds through the November election, the decision effectively meant no money for ads in August. Remembering how they had run out of money in the Gore campaign in 2000, Devine and Shrum wanted to save their limited war chest for a media blitz in late October—at the end, when it really counted. But that left little or no ammo to shoot back at the Swift Boat vets in August.

Shrum would later insist that he saw the need to take action soon after the Swift Boat ads began cutting into support for Kerry in August. Still, the media men lacked a certain imagination, or at least gumption, about pushing back. In late August the campaign finally made a small media buy to answer the Swifties, but it was like using a fly swatter against an elephant.

Kerry was unhappy with Devine and Shrum, but he was not about to fire them. Shrum was his old friend, his peer; besides, Kerry procrastinated for as long as possible before firing anyone. As he fretted and moped, his eye fell on other, less independently powerful figures in the campaign. He was particularly annoyed at Stephanie Cutter, the communications director. In a crowded press room, Cutter was easy to spot with her dirty-blond hair and high boots, as she lectured some sheepish or irked newsperson. Cutter had been the object of endless complaining by reporters and campaign staffers. She was considered too slow and too controlling, not nimble or clever. Tired of watching her berate interns and alienate reporters with vituperative e-mails after the most mildly critical stories, a few Kerry staffers snidely made a verb of her e-mail name (scutter@johnkerry.com). "To Scutter" meant to try to control or dominate. Its second meaning was cruder, "to f— something up." In March reporters had begun to vent about Cutter to campaign manager Mary Beth Cahill. By May they were taking their grievances to Kerry himself. In July Kerry said to Cahill, "I'm tired of hearing complaints about Stephanie. Fix it."

CAHILL HAD ALREADY MOVED Cutter out of headquarters and onto the campaign plane. The idea was to marginalize her by confining her duties. But Cutter was a skillful bureaucratic infighter. She managed to keep sway over communications at headquarters in Washington and at the same time run the press operation on the plane. If anything, she was expanding her empire. She insisted that everything—all campaign communications—had to go through her, effectively slowing down response time to a crawl. (After the election, Cutter rejected this characterization as wrong. "I was asked to go on the plane to provide some message discipline to Kerry—the press operation was not working. I took myself out of message development. I do have regrets about this period, such as not beefing up rapid response.")

Cutter could be tough-minded, and some of her instincts were sound. Democrats are notoriously loose-lipped and leaky. Cutter was trying to impose some Republican-like message discipline, to be a sort of Democratic Karen Hughes. But she lacked the kind of gravitas and seasoned judgment to play such a role. She was notoriously jealous of rivals. In the spring Hillary Clinton's former press secretary, Howard Wolfson, had signed on to work with Cutter on campaign communications. He lasted all of two and a half days; he had gone to lunch on a Wednesday and never come back.

Cutter reported to Mary Beth Cahill. It was Cahill's job to see that Cutter worked out—or to make a change. But Cahill's own authority was becoming shaky. Kerry had never regarded her as much of a strategist, but he had been grateful for her hands-on, no-excuses management style when, in the fall of 2003, she had left her post as Ted Kennedy's chief of staff to rescue the floundering Kerry campaign. But over time Cahill had lost her effectiveness. Back in December she had succeeded in turning off Kerry's cell phone, curtailing the candidate's weakness for back-channeling and second-guessing. But Kerry's cell-phone addiction was hard to break, and within a few weeks he was dialing his dozens of campaign advisers and kibitzers all day and much of the night.

Cutter became a symbol of Cahill's power, a test case of the campaign manager's increasingly precarious grip. Staffers could not quite understand Cahill's solicitude for the much-maligned Cutter. In late August, one campaign adviser wondered why, if the future of the Kerry campaign and possibly the nation was at stake, everyone was so worried about hurting the feelings of Stephanie Cutter.

The most intense grumbling about the sorry state of the Kerry campaign came from the so-called Clintonistas. The followers and former aides of President Bill Clinton had been the masters of rapid response, the creators of the much-mythologized 1992 war room that never let a news cycle pass without a charge rebutted. The Clinton team was also the only Democratic political faction to actually win any presidential elections over the previous quarter century.

Not unreasonably, the Clintonistas felt a certain standing to pronounce judgment and offer critiques.

THE LOUDEST, and most colorful, sideline commentator was James Carville, the Ragin' Cajun, who, along with his peppery Republican wife, Mary Matalin, had become a kind of media-political institution in Washington. Carville (affectionately known by his wife as "Ol' Serpent Head") could be heard cheerfully squawking and blathering on CNN's "Crossfire" and at pretty much any cocktail party where prominent journalists and political consultants gathered. For a time Carville uncharacteristically restrained himself with Kerry. The two men talked on the phone, but the earthy Carville and the Brahmin Kerry were not natural soul mates. In the spring, Carville had urged Kerry to bring on his buddy and "Crossfire" cohost Paul Begala to help with strategy and campaign communications. An amiable, fast-talking Texan, Begala had helped out Kerry for a couple of weeks, but the two did not click. Kerry signaled to Cahill that Begala was not the campaign sidekick he was looking for (inviting the question of whether Kerry, the loner, really wanted such a companion in the first place). Cahill did not directly tell Begala it was a no-go, but she stopped returning his phone calls. Left hanging, Begala felt wounded. Carville hurt for his pal, and began having a harder time holding his tongue about the failings of the Kerry campaign.

In August Joe Lockhart, President Clinton's last White House press secretary, joined the campaign plane to bolster

Cutter and bring some energy and action to the slow-footed communications department. Lockhart had the idea of sending Max Cleland, the former senator from Georgia who had lost three limbs in Vietnam, on a mission. Cleland was dispatched, in his wheelchair, to the gates of the Bush ranch in Crawford, Texas, to deliver a letter calling on Bush to renounce the Swifties' smear campaign. The stunt, while gimmicky, at least showed some pluck. But it did not move the polls, which were sinking fast for Kerry.

During the Republican convention Kerry repaired to Teresa's house on Nantucket. He had bounced around between his marriages, renting small apartments, bunking on the couches of friends. Teresa had called it her husband's "homeless period." Of Teresa's five houses (Washington, Boston, Sun Valley, Pittsburgh, Nantucket), Kerry seemed to feel most at home at the heiress's weathered, shingled "cottage" with its wide porches overlooking Nantucket Harbor. He went windsurfing, inviting along press photographers. This was a mistake: he was effectively providing the Republicans with more ammunition to portray him as effete and overprivileged, indulging in rich man's play (and—even more devastating—affording the perfect video of Kerry symbolically tacking back and forth in the political winds). But mostly, in the last days of August, he disappeared inside, away from his staff. A silence descended over the candidate, a disturbing, distant quiet. His aides looked at his stony stare and tried to read his mind. They wondered, was he back in Vietnam?

Teresa just seemed fed up. She had been initially reluctant to see her husband run for president. "First Lady?" she would ask. "No, thanks!" Her protest had seemed coy to some at the time, but after the election, Kerry insisted that Teresa had been sincere. According to Kerry, she had told her first husband, Sen. John Heinz, that she didn't want him to run for president, and she had initially opposed Kerry's own campaign. Feeling the call of duty and history, she had rallied to her husband's cause. Indeed, she had become an active and aggressive strategist. That is, she had tried to be. But too often, she found, her ideas went unheeded.

At least Bob Shrum had been polite about it. The ever-courtly Shrum had flattered her and seemed to listen before rejecting her advice, and then did so ever so gently and almost never directly to her face. But Mary Beth Cahill lacked Shrum's tact or subtle gifts. With her unvarnished manner, Cahill appeared annoyed by any meddling from the candidate's wife. Teresa, for her part, decided that Cahill was arrogant, and the two strong-willed women clashed, most openly when Cahill rejected Teresa's nomination for a new press aide in June. Kerry was caught in the middle. If he sided with his staff, as he usually did because he had more regard for their advice, he risked an unpleasant argument with his wife. All through the disastrous "Sea to Shining Sea" tour in July and August, she had complained of one thing or another and he had tried to mollify her without stirring trouble with the staff. Now, as the campaign entered the fall stretch, Teresa was visibly tired of it all. She still badly wanted to beat Bush, she told her close friends and family.

But she was looking forward to getting away from politics and spending time with her kids.

Kerry was brooding, pondering a move. He didn't want to fire Cahill or Cutter, in part because it would set off another round of Kerry-campaign-in-disarray stories and feed the impression, already starting to take hold in the press, that he was a poor manager. But he was at last ready to shove Cutter to the side, and to undercut Cahill's authority.

Kerry was still stewing over the blunder at the Grand Canyon on Aug. 9, when he had disastrously affirmed that he would have voted to give the president the authority to invade Iraq, WMD or not. At the time, adviser Jamie Rubin had taken the fall. But within the campaign, fingers were pointing at Cutter for failing to quickly straighten out the mess. Conveniently overlooking his own responsibility, Kerry blamed Cutter for the consequences—the Republican ads crowing that flip-floppin' Kerry was now backing the president on Iraq.

It was Carville who led the charge against Cahill and Cutter. Carville had been feeling guilty, fretful that he had not directly confronted the Kerry campaign with its failings. On the last weekend in August, the old Clinton alumni gathered in the backyard of a former embassy off 16th Street to celebrate the wedding of Gene Sperling, Clinton's former economic adviser. After a few drinks, the celebration veered toward becoming a wake for the Kerry campaign. Carville, in particular, was in a high state of agitation, going around telling anyone who would listen what a mess the campaign had become.

Carville was working himself up to a confrontation. On the Saturday morning of Labor Day weekend, with the Republicans basking in the success of their convention, he decided to try to force the issue. Along with Clinton's old pollster Stan Greenberg, Carville went to see Mary Beth Cahill and Joe Lockhart at the Kerry campaign headquarters on 15th Street. Greenberg was soft-spoken and generally supportive of the Kerry team, though he did offer a critique demonstrating that Kerry's speeches sounded about five different themes without any organizing principle. Carville, however, was so worked up that he began to cry. He wanted so badly to beat Bush, he said, yet the Kerry campaign was failing miserably. Carville came right out and said that Cahill had to step aside and let Lockhart, the Clintonista newcomer, run the campaign. "You've got to let him do it!" implored Carville, pounding Lockhart's arm until it was bruised. Carville spoke as if Mary Beth weren't in the room. "Nobody can gain power without someone losing power. If somebody doesn't lose power, nobody's gained power," he lectured. The "somebody" sitting a few feet away just remained silent. Carville threatened to go on "Meet the Press" the next day "and tell the truth about how bad it is" if Cahill didn't give effective control to Lockhart.

Cahill and all the others later dressed up the truth—it had been her idea, they said, to bring in Lockhart and other old Clinton aides to strengthen the campaign. After the election, Kerry somewhat gingerly described the power shift—and his own role behind it. "She reached out to these people," he said. "I urged her to broaden the base."

The most prominent Clintonista also weighed in that Saturday, Sept. 4. Former President Clinton was resting in a hospital bed in New York City, awaiting a heart-bypass operation, when Kerry called him, as he periodically did to solicit advice. Clinton couldn't resist injecting himself into the Kerry campaign crisis. For 90 minutes that night, as various campaign aides listened in on a conference call, the ex-president lectured the would-be president on what he had to do to get back in the race. Clinton urged Kerry to spend less time talking about Vietnam and more time engaging on Iraq. This was not the first time Clinton had weighed in. Some of the suggestions were a little over the top, the Kerry aides thought. In an earlier phone call, Clinton—ever the political triangulator, looking for ways to pick up swing voters by reaching into the so-called Red States—had urged Kerry to back a constitutional ban on gay marriage. Kerry respectfully listened, then told his aides, "I'm not going to ever do that." (Kerry did support some local bans on gay marriage.)

On Monday morning, less than 36 hours later, Kerry read a none-too-flattering account of his phone call with Clinton on the front page of *The New York Times*. The article made both Clinton and Kerry look a little desperate, engaged in a sickbed séance over Kerry's political survival. The imagery was demoralizing: if Kerry was so hapless at running his own campaign, voters were going to start wondering how well he would run the White House. Kerry was furious and chewed out Lockhart, whom he suspected to be the source. Not true, insisted Lockhart, still new on the job but already on the verge of quitting (others suspected Carville of the leak; he denied it). Kerry was beleaguered. He was wary of the agenda of the Clinton exiles: if he lost in November, the way would be open for Hillary Clinton to run for president in 2008.

K ERRY'S SMALL CIRCLE felt surrounded, besieged, cut off. The campaign had made much of contesting more than 20 swing states. But one of those battleground states, Missouri, already seemed lost. On Sept. 9 Alex Kerry traveled there with her father. At a Kerry rally she decided to try to find out what "real people" thought by asking a few of them. A group of Democratic voters didn't recognize her. Encouraged by her anonymity, she crossed the street to talk to some Republican protesters. "We know who you are," one of them spat out. Others began shouting that her father was a "baby killer." Shocked by their vehemence, she went to find her father, who quickly saw how upset his daughter had become. He cleared the room of aides. Alex dissolved in tears. "What if they steal the election?" she cried. "We're not going to let that happen," Kerry tried to reassure her. Alex was feeling more and more isolated. Her friends tried to console her, telling her, "Everything will be all right." But she didn't believe them.

Kerry's top consultants weren't having a much better time of it. Tad Devine trooped up to Capitol Hill the week after Labor Day to hear the complaints of Democratic congressmen, who were fearful that the whole party would suffer in November, that any hope of regaining control of the House was fast disappearing. As Devine tried to buck them up, he noticed that congressmen were getting up and walking out. He heard bells ringing, and assumed, or rather hoped, that they were leaving to go vote on the House floor. They weren't. They were just showing their contempt for the Kerry campaign.

Bob Shrum was brooding over a rough profile in the Style section of *The Washington Post*. Shrum generally got good press, in part because he was a source and friend to so many top political journalists. But this article went on about the "Shrum Curse," his 0-for-7 record in presidential races, and revealed that Kerry staffers wanted to make up T-shirts reading BREAK THE SHRUM CURSE. The story dwelled on gritty details, like Shrum's habit of parking his Nicorette gum on the rim of Diet Coke cans. Shrum was wounded and wanted to find the campaign mole. He recovered after a few days, but his friends wondered if he might not disengage from the campaign and fade into the background.

At Kerry headquarters on McPherson Square, quiet gloom had settled in. By the end of the summer the campaign was sponsoring cocktail happy hours, encouraging the troops to go to a local bar and put on a glow before coming back for a long night of work. But the drinking had taken a melancholy turn; the mood had a "last hurrah" feel to it. Young staffers who once dreamed of a job in the White House were now wondering what they might do after Nov. 2.

On the Tuesday after Labor Day, a special guest slipped in. Ted Kennedy didn't want it known by the press that he was visiting Kerry headquarters; the campaign had been careful to keep the very symbol of Massachusetts liberalism at arm's length. Kennedy had heard the staff was dispirited, and he wanted to give them a pep talk. He told how his brother Jack had played through pain during the 1936 football season at Harvard. Turning red in the face, he shouted, "In the next two months I want you to fight harder than you'll ever fight!" The staffers roared. Morale improved, at least a little.

The real boost came when Joe Lockhart took over the campaign's communications and "message" from Cutter and Shrum. Every morning at 7:15 Lockhart held a meeting for top staffers. The topic was always the same: "What headline do we want and how do we go about getting it?" Lockhart wanted, in classic Clinton fashion, to start winning the news cycle of the day. The Republicans had been beating the Democrats at their own game of rapid response. Lockhart was going to win back the franchise.

In the beginning of the last week of September, Kerry went on the offensive about Iraq. The war was getting much worse again. There had been a lull (in the fighting but especially in the news coverage) after the United States had handed over authority to an interim Iraqi government on June 30. But in July, August and September, casualties steadily climbed, and the fighting bled back onto the front pages. Former Clinton pollster Stan Greenberg had been pressing Kerry to tie the war to domestic needs—to declare that $200 billion spent on Iraq meant that much less funding for education and health care at home. Kerry used the line in a few speeches, but reluctantly. He didn't really believe it. In truth, he was willing to spend whatever it took to win in Iraq, or at least to extricate the United States with some semblance of honor.

Still, he was appalled by the carnage in Iraq and the waste of the war. On Sunday night, Sept. 19, the campaign staff met to discuss, one more time, the candidate's position on Iraq. The Clintonistas pushed a harder line against the war. But the campaign's old guard wasn't so sure. Couldn't Kerry play it both ways? Shrum cautioned against appearing too dovish. Kerry seemed to let the debate go on, circling around and around.

But then he spoke. "It's gut-check time, folks," he said. "This is not about whether it's politically expedient. This is a f—ing war. Kids are dying out there, and this president continues not to tell the truth. You'd have to be out of your mind to go in there the way he did. There was no WMD, no imminent threat, no ties to Al Qaeda. The answer is no. Anything else is crap."

Kerry knew he had not been getting through on Iraq, that he was regarded as equivocal or basically no different from Bush. He was mad at the press for being obtuse and easily manipulated by the Bush campaign, but he also knew he had himself to blame. The next day he gave a blistering speech at NYU, attacking Bush for the folly of invading Iraq. The Bush campaign had some fun with an ad showing Kerry tacking back and forth on his windsurfer. But to campaign staffers desperate for some sign that Kerry was turning a corner— that the famous fourth-quarter player had finally taken the field—he sounded convincing.

For months Kerry had been the oldest political person on his campaign plane by about 20 years. He may have liked to be a loner, playing his guitar and watching old movies, but he needed a grown-up to advise him and deliver bad news if necessary. John Sasso had been Kerry's original choice as campaign manager in 2002. A much-sought-after consultant to private businesses, Sasso had been unwilling to drop all his clients and join the campaign. After Kerry locked up the nomination in February, Sasso took a job at the Democratic National Committee running the party's get-out-the-vote operation, which allowed him to play part-time adviser to the Kerry campaign. An old Boston hand, Sasso was a gut player. He didn't always win (he had been brought in, too late, to try to salvage the sinking Dukakis campaign in 1988), but he had good instincts and wasn't intimidated by Kerry's intellectualism. In September, Sasso started traveling with Kerry. When the nominee began to complain that he was losing his voice only a week before the first debate, Sasso saw an opening. He took away Kerry's cell phone. "You need to rest your voice, Senator. I'll tell you if there are any messages you need to know about." Kerry grumbled, but he went along.

The other new player on the plane was Mike McCurry. One of the best-liked White House press secretaries, McCurry had weathered the Lewinsky scandal and the chaos of the Clinton years with a wry smile and a deft touch with reporters. His relaxed demeanor starkly contrasted with Stephanie Cutter's hard edge. Kerry had tried to hire McCurry back in the spring of 2004, but he, too, had been unwilling to give up all his private clients, and campaign manager Cahill (possibly sensing a rival) had insisted on all or nothing. Now everyone agreed that McCurry's soothing presence was critical. Typically, McCurry joked that he had given up an easy and well-paid life to go to work for his former subordinate—Joe Lockhart, who had been his deputy at the White House before succeeding him.

WITH THE NEW TEAM ONBOARD, the campaign actually began to win a few rounds of the battle for cable-news supremacy, the daily struggle over who can control the 24/7 airwaves of CNN, Fox and MSNBC. But, somewhat disturbingly, the candidate would improve—then regress. He was sharp and tough in his prepared speeches on the war. But at a town meeting in the Wisconsin hamlet of Spring Green in late September, the old Kerry was on full display. He rambled about, wreathed in nuance, as he puzzled then lost his audience. Seeking to be all things to all people, he tried to be empathetic about rising college tuition. He earnestly told the crowd that he knew how hard it was to find the right financial options because he had two children and three stepchildren. His audience, mostly farmers and laborers and small businessmen, audibly laughed at him. Kerry was married to a billionaire, right? What did he know about making ends meet?

The town meeting was Kerry's only public appearance that week. The campaign was preparing for the first of three presidential debates. It was obvious that Kerry could not afford to lose any of them, and certainly not the first. For several weeks Kerry had been demanding more debate-prep time. He would take practice questions, sometimes for hours, and then go off and write. This exercise was, generally speaking, beneficial. Kerry usually stuck to the script when he wrote it himself. But he deviated and wandered when he was using someone else's words. Still, his aides worried when the candidate disappeared to his room for the night. Was he living in some kind of bubble, a fantasy land? Would he ignore the professional advice of his handlers? Kerry would summon an aide from time to time to go over the debate books, but to his staff the candidate seemed solitary, alone, again.

Squaring off: Just before the first round in Miami

(Photo by David Hume Kennerly / Getty Images for *Newsweek*)

SEVEN

The Debates:
Face to Face

*Kerry was finally back in the game
after his skillful performance.*

THE BC04 HIGH COMMAND, Karl Rove and Karen
Hughes and their top aides, watched the first debate on TV monitors set up inside a racquetball
court at the University of Miami's Wellness Center. They
failed to see that their candidate was losing. Mostly, they
were waiting, and hoping, for Kerry to say something that
could be used against him. When, late in the debate, the
Democratic candidate accommodated by rambling on about
a "global test" that America must pass before intervening
abroad, Rove exulted, "Oh, my God!" He could visualize TV
commercials that could be fed to Red State Americans who
were suspicious of the United Nations and regarded Kerry
as vaguely French.

Hughes, however, was bothered. She observed that NBC

appeared to be putting the president on a split screen whenever Kerry spoke. The ground rules for the debate expressly forbade "reaction shots," but the Bush team knew that the networks would ignore that stipulation. The president had been warned. Still, Hughes was irritated at the frequency of the split screen, and she could see right away that one of the ground rules had been a mistake. The podiums were each 50 inches high, but since Kerry was at least five inches taller than Bush, on the screen the president appeared to be peering over the rostrum like a schoolboy at a candy counter. Hughes also noticed that Bush appeared to be fidgeting and grimacing. She made a face. "I wish he wouldn't do that," she said, to no one in particular.

THE OTHERS SAID NOTHING. Rove didn't even notice the president's grimace. They had all seen it before, almost every day. That was the way the president was, charming and funny sometimes, but also caustic and petulant and impatient. His aides were accustomed to his moods. Bush never let anyone doubt that he was in charge, and his subordinates admired him for it. They always quieted and stood when he came into a room. If Bush seemed a little entitled, well, he was entitled. He was president—a war president. Bush was mostly from Midland, Texas, but he still had a touch of Greenwich, Conn., in him. He was a legacy of an aristocratic family, grandson of a senator, son of a president, born to rule. His father, normally the most gracious of men, had sometimes explained himself by saying, "Because I'm president and you're not." George W didn't put it that way. But his body language did.

Later some of his aides would wonder, maybe he had become a little too sure of his essential, unchallenged, unassailable rightness of being. Among his advisers, who stood up to him, really? Hughes, maybe, but she was usually deferential and called him "sir." Rove would hold forth and dominate discussion, but the president still reminded him of his subordinate status with jokey nicknames ("Turd Blossom"). In the debate prep, Sen. Judd Gregg of New Hampshire had played the role of Kerry. He was supposed to get under Bush's skin, and he tried to assume the mien of a reserved New England WASP. But while tall and lanky and reserved like Kerry, he lacked Kerry's frosty air of superiority. He just didn't inspire in Bush the same feelings of resentment and lip-curling contempt that Kerry did.

To prepare the president for the debates and to soften the ground before him, a vast machine had churned away. In fluorescent-lit cubicles at RNC headquarters in Washington, the "oppo" (opposition) research team had spent months poring over tapes of Kerry's past debates. Working amid black filing cabinets and workstations adorned with inspirational tabloid headlines like KERRY SEX DISEASE SCANDAL, the moles of RNC oppo research analyzed Kerry's body language, looking for weaknesses to exploit. They found few. The oppo team produced a thick binder titled "2004 John Kerry Debate Analysis," and researchers concluded that he had been a remarkably consistent debater over the years, respectful but aggressive, rarely hitting home runs but rarely striking out. Kerry's vanquished opponent from Massachusetts, former governor Bill Weld, was summoned to give testimony. He told the Bushies that Kerry had "the nerve of a burglar," that he would coolly say anything and get away with it. Rove and Hughes just listened to Weld without saying a word.

A legal team of GOP heavyweights led by former secretary of State James Baker had negotiated 32 pages of strict rules. The Bushies wanted to limit answers to two minutes, figuring that the windy Kerry would run over, while banning direct questions between the candidates. Bush's advisers worried that Kerry, the Yale debating champ, might somehow outfox the former Deke House rush chairman. The Democrats were represented by the equally formidable Democratic superlawyer Vernon Jordan. Campaign operatives joked that the two old Washington hands could settle their differences with a golf round at Burning Tree, an exclusive all-male country club. Each side made concessions: the Republicans agreed to three instead of two debates, and the Democrats allowed the first debate to be solely on foreign policy, supposedly Bush's strong suit.

None of this jockeying mattered much. Nor did the substantive issues, really. Vast numbers of Americans watched the debates—more than 62 million on the first night, about 35 percent more than tuned in for the first Bush-Gore debate in 2000. The experts gravely intoned that 9/11 had raised the stakes, but it may just be that the debates had become like reality TV, "Survivor" or "The Apprentice" for politicians.

The Bush team had gone in cocky. The night before the

Miami debate, at a birthday party for press aide Steve Schmidt at a fancy South Beach bar, a couple of Bush aides twirled their cigars as they chatted up reporters. Professional pessimist Matthew Dowd had been going on about Kerry as the "best debater since Cicero," but most BC04 operatives believed their own propaganda, that Kerry was a windbag and a loser. Bush himself had tried to keep the atmosphere light at debate prep (held after 9 P.M. to acclimate the president, who normally liked to go to bed no later than 10). Bush kept a running gag going about respect for his dog, Barney. When the terrier entered the room, Bush would command, "All rise." The president's aides would dutifully stand. Bush's daughters started joking that their father loved his dog more than them.

Adman Mark McKinnon convinced himself that the president was ready. "He's in the zone," McKinnon began e-mailing reporters. "He's really loose, he's ready," McKinnon said to White House Communications Director Dan Bartlett shortly before the debate. "Eh, not so sure about that," muttered Bartlett. The president actually seemed tight and a little tired from pressing the flesh that morning with hurricane-weary Floridians.

IN THE PRESS ROOM watching the debate, the White House regulars, the beat reporters from the big dailies like *The Washington Post* and *The New York Times* and the major networks, did not notice anything unusual about the president's demeanor or body language. (They were watching a live feed from the debate hall, not the network's coverage, so they did not see split-screen reaction shots.) They, too, had seen him smirk and pout, sometimes as a gag, sometimes because he was genuinely irked. But among the punditocracy, the talking heads of cable TV who rendered judgment, thumbs up or down, the conventional wisdom quickly congealed: Bush had been as whiny and wriggly as a spoiled child. Kerry had been cool and calm. Dignified. Presidential.

In Spin Alley, where campaign officials, beneath signposts announcing their names, parried with jostling reporters, the Bush team might as well have been trying to beat back the tide. "I don't think he sounded defensive," said Dowd, sounding defensive. "I didn't see irritation," said Bartlett. The reporters hooted. "Would you say that this is the president's worst debate performance?" demanded Vince Morris of the *New York Post*, the conservative Rupert Murdoch tabloid that could normally be relied on to boost Bush.

At first the BC04 team blamed the liberal bias of the mainstream press or the media's horse-race obsession. The press needed to close the gap, to make Kerry look like the Comeback Kid, the Bushies rationalized. The laws of media physics required that the race tighten. Kerry had looked presidential just by mounting the same stage as President Bush.

There was some truth to these excuses, but the state of denial soon wore off. Not officially: at BC04 headquarters, where only good news and positive thinking were tolerated, the first debate was treated like the crazy uncle in the attic, a subject not to be mentioned in polite company. But the consultants and midlevel aides traded furtive e-mails and subversive jokes. One Bush adman, Fred Davis, pointed out in an e-mail to ad chieftain McKinnon that the news wasn't all bad: people who heard the debate on the radio thought Bush had won. To be sure, that had been Richard Nixon's excuse when he sweatily lost to John F. Kennedy in the very first televised debate, in 1960. McKinnon dryly replied, "Working to make the next debate radio only."

The cocky mood among the top brass evaporated within about 24 hours. The backslapping and high-fives gave way to a kind of focused grimness and some quiet backbiting. Karen Hughes was especially feeling the heat. It had been chiefly her responsibility to get Bush up for the debate, to soften his edges and keep him in the groove. Now her colleagues were quietly grumbling that she had allowed Bush to be overprepared, that too many advisers had been in his face offering too much last-minute coaching, overloading and confusing him. Bush had been told to use the full two minutes allotted to answer. At times he had seemed to be filibustering, as if he had run out of things to say and was just filling air time.

With her reputation on the line, Hughes let it be known to the press that she, at least, had been the one to speak truth to power after the debate. Bush had naturally dismissed post-debate criticism as the nattering of press nabobs. "I was not irritated," he protested to Hughes. "Sir, you were," replied Hughes, according to an account leaked to *Time* magazine.

The one person who had always leveled with Bush was his wife, Laura. It had been Laura who, many years earlier, had delivered an ultimatum to her husband when he was drinking heavily: "It's either the Jim Beam or me." Now she said to him, "I don't know what happened. You've got to be yourself, and you weren't."

The problem was that Bush had been himself. Not the teasing, playful, warm man he could be, but the peevish, hyper man he also was. He had shown his true feelings toward Kerry. His whole body and manner cried out that he was a president with a war to fight who didn't want to be bothered trading verbal jabs with the kind of supercilious know-it-all he had loathed since Yale days.

Mississippi Gov. Haley Barbour, an old friend of the Bush family's and a former head of the Republican Party, had watched the debate on TV from his house in Yazoo City, Miss. Barbour could see clearly what millions of Americans saw or felt: the president looked as if he didn't want to be there.

In the racquetball court at the University of Miami Wellness Center reserved for the Kerry-Edwards team, the cheering was loud and raucous. "He's crushing him!" cried out Bob Shrum repeatedly. Wearing his trademark good-luck scarf, feeling the three-decade-old weight of the Shrum curse, Kerry's speechwriter (and still friend) was wired tight. When Kerry veered off into a discussion of the Kyoto Protocol, Shrum threw down his cell phone. But at the end of the debate he was ecstatic, like all of Kerry's aides. They rushed to the motorcade to make the victory celebration before the 11 o'clock news, and they were waiting for the candidate when he stepped from his limousine. As they stood applauding, Kerry smiled and administered hugs.

The campaign pollsters, as well as the TV networks, had hired focus groups, drawn from undecided or committed voters, to watch the debate and twist the dials of applause meters every time one candidate or another gave an answer. In an Amsterdam hotel room, where it was after 3 A.M., pollster Stan Greenberg watched technology confirm what he had thought, viewing the debate from half a world away. On his laptop the dial numbers were jumping for Kerry. Jubilant, Greenberg, who was in Europe to make a speech, caught a 5:30 A.M. cab and headed for the airport to catch a plane back home.

ONE KERRY ADVISER, John Sasso, was already thinking about the second debate, to be held in St. Louis on Oct. 8. "All we did was get back in the game," said Sasso. "There's nothing to be giddy about." One debate did not mean victory, he cautioned. Sasso continued to be a steadying hand on the campaign plane. Staffers called him "the Wolf," after the character, played by Harvey Keitel, who comes in and quietly but methodically cleans up the mess in the movie *Pulp Fiction*.

Kerry and Sasso made an odd couple. Sasso was the grandson of Italian immigrants from New Jersey, more at home in a local union hall than in Kerry's home on Beacon Hill. Sasso stood out from the hip young campaign staffers. Conservatively dressed in a white shirt and tie, the short, stocky Sasso was low-key but direct with Kerry: "You've got to do this in 10 minutes instead of 20," he'd say as Kerry took the stage for a speech. Insofar as he was capable of obeying any-one's advice to shorten his speeches, Kerry heeded Sasso. The two men were the same age, and peers: Sasso had been Gov. Michael Dukakis's chief of staff when Kerry was lieu-tenant governor back in the early 1980s.

Though the arrival of Sasso on the plane and the interven-tion of the Clintonistas was seen as a slap to campaign man-ager Mary Beth Cahill, she was relieved to have Sasso onboard. She had become overwhelmed, unable to run headquarters and the plane, too. (Cahill was defensive about her protégée Stephanie Cutter, but she acknowledged that Cutter was over her head trying to manage both the cam-paign "message" and rapid response.) She appreciated Sasso's impact on the chronically late Kerry. When Sasso "says, 'C'mon, we're going,' it's harder for Kerry to say, 'Not yet,'" said Cahill. But even Sasso was not able to keep Kerry's cell phone away from him. Despite Al Gore's admonition to stop dialing up kibitzers—"You have what you have, you can't take any more advice," Gore told him—Kerry was back on his cell after the first debate.

Sasso, who had last run a presidential campaign in 1988, warned Kerry, "I'm rusty." But he was better than anyone else at diagnosing the candidate's problems and fixing them, or trying to. Sasso had sensed that something was seriously wrong with the Kerry organization back in August. When he came aboard in September, he found a candidate who had turned himself into a pincushion. Dazed and dispirited by the sorry state of his campaign, Kerry had been inviting personal criticism from pretty much anyone who had an opinion. The critics had unloaded on him, and then they didn't let up. By the time he reached out to Sasso, Kerry was drowning in negative energy from all around.

Sasso wanted it to stop. He put out the word that there was to be no more direct criticism of the candidate, period. Complaints should be directed to Sasso and no further. Teresa was not exempt. Sasso told her that she was being too hard on her husband. "He needs to be optimistic and focused," Sasso told her. That couldn't happen if his wife was eternally whispering in his ear. Teresa got the message and promised to back off. Alex and Vanessa also spent less time cajoling and critiquing their father and more time giving him breaks for humor and affection. The girls provided him with running reports on a 14-foot great white shark that had swum into the shallow inlet at Naushon, the privately owned island off the coast of Massachusetts where Kerry had taught them how to swim many years before. While his campaign struggled to survive, Kerry was happy to obsess with his girls about the shark in the swimming hole.

DEBATE PREP FOR KERRY had gone badly at first. In early September, Kerry staged a mock debate for a focus group that twisted dials to measure his performance. The numbers were low; he had been defensive, all about himself and not about the voters. With his relentless self-criticism, he crammed harder (his briefing book was even fatter than policy wonk Al Gore's in 2000, "and that's saying something," noted a veteran aide). Advisers tried to think up clever lines.

Congressman Barney Frank suggested that Kerry deadpan to Bush, "I used to get really upset about how much you distort my record until I heard how much you distort your own." But quips and one-liners really weren't Kerry's style, so he decided to give up attempts at humor. To cure him of his long-windedness and teach him to keep his answers under two minutes, Kerry's handlers brought in the biggest, loudest buzzer they could find, "something between electroshock therapy and the electric fence for dogs," said debate coach Michael Sheehan. Sheehan worked with the candidate to "get positive" during the last 30 seconds of his answer. The switch from slashing his opponent to presenting his own vision was called "the clubhouse turn."

Sheehan wasn't even in the same city when Kerry debated. Speech coaches are not supposed to be seen by the press. Shrum, however, paraded by reporters in a Boston hotel on his way to debate prep in Spring Green, Wis., as if to underscore that rumors of his demise had been exaggerated. Shrum had worked his way back into Kerry's favor with his expert debate coaching (like Kerry, he had been a champion debater in college). Kerry was grateful to Shrum for not engaging in public feuds with his rivals and detractors (it had been rumored in the press that Shrum was being shoved aside even from his specialty, debate prep). "Bob, we've just got to get to Nov. 2," Kerry had implored him over the phone. "We can talk about this on Nov. 3."

Allotted 45 minutes for the predebate "walkthrough" in Miami, Kerry took 43, asking to see a "freeze frame" of him standing at the podium, engaging in earnest debate over neckties. (Blue? No, Bush wore blue ties. Red? Yes, but not too bright . . .) Bush, by contrast, breezed through in 10 minutes.

To play the part of Bush in debate prep, the Kerry team brought in Gregory Craig, a skillful Washington litigator who could imitate Bush's slow speaking style but think very quickly on his feet. Craig was slicing up Kerry for his double-speak and his infamous voted-for-and-against "flip-flop" on Iraq, when Kerry, frustrated, stopped the practice session. "I can't believe I'm getting killed over a stupid thing I said, and this guy has totally screwed up the war—and he's not paying a price for it," he blurted out. Kerry's outburst became the foundation for his most effective debate line: "I made a mistake in how I talk about the war. But the president made a mistake in invading Iraq. Which is worse?"

On the defensive for most of the past two months, Kerry was looking for a way to turn the tables on Bush. For most of the campaign, he had shied from trying to make a campaign issue out of Osama bin Laden's escape from his mountain hideout in Tora Bora in December 2001. The campaign's fear was that the United States would capture bin Laden before the election, trumping Kerry. But Ron Klain, a veteran Democratic operative brought in to help prep Kerry for the debates, argued that it was a mistake to just leave such a big arrow sitting in the quiver. He urged Kerry to pound Bush on the failure to bring bin Laden to justice. It was a way of sharpening Kerry's larger criticism, that Bush was fighting the wrong war by invading Iraq. The real enemy was bin Laden and Al Qaeda, not Saddam Hussein and Iraq. At the debate, Kerry's harping on bin Laden worked perfectly to enrage Bush. "Of course, I know it was bin Laden who attacked us," Bush spluttered.

Kerry also infuriated Bush by playing the daddy card. "You know," Kerry intoned, "the president's father did not go into Iraq, into Baghdad beyond Basra. And the reason he didn't is, he said, he wrote in his book, because there was no viable exit strategy. And he said our troops would be occupiers in a bitterly hostile land. That's exactly where we find ourselves today." Kerry's remarks were a conscious ploy, a rehearsed setup designed to get Bush's goat, according to one member of Kerry's inner circle. Klain and Cahill deny that Kerry was consciously aiming at Bush's adolescent id, but they say they were happily surprised when Bush seemed flummoxed by the reference to his father.

Some of Kerry's advisers were hoping that he could play the daddy card again when the candidates faced off in a "town meeting" in St. Louis. But on Oct. 7, the day before that second debate, *New York Times* columnist Maureen Dowd, a keen observer of Bush family psychodramas, wrote a column titled "Getting Junior's Goat." Dowd strongly suggested that Kerry had intentionally played an Oedipal trick on the president and planned to do it again in St. Louis. "Mr. Kerry may take on the voice of Daddy Bush again in Friday's domestic debate," she wrote. One furious staffer in Kerry's inner circle fired off a memo to Sasso and Joe Lockhart on the campaign plane titled, "Who Leaked to Maureen Dowd?" Dowd's column intimated that the Clintonistas had taken credit for the ploy.

To some Kerry loyalists a pattern was emerging. Every time the campaign did something smart, an item would appear in the press crediting the intervention of the Clintonistas. Some of the paid Kerry staffers saw greed at work. Lockhart, McCurry, Carville and Begala were all burnishing their reputations as PR geniuses who could save any campaign, even John Kerry's. The payoff would be higher fees for them in future campaigns or from private clients.

Staffers on the Edwards for Vice President plane were especially wary of the Clintonistas. If Kerry lost, Edwards would be vying with Hillary Clinton for the Democratic nomination in 2008. When a *New York Times* article suggested that Edwards was not fulfilling the attack-dog role of veep candidates in order to preserve his sunny image, the Edwards aides immediately fingered the Clintonistas as the sources. The Kerry communications office, now under Clintonista management, urged Edwards to say that the Republican convention reminded him of the movie *Grumpy Old Men*. An Edwards aide responded, "It's a great line. You should use it."

The Edwards camp expected Vice President Dick Cheney to try to savage the Kerry-Edwards ticket in the vice presidential debate on Oct. 5. "He's going to come in with a machine gun," said Shrum, who was helping to prepare Edwards. The Edwardses' 6-year-old daughter Emma Claire was standing nearby, listening. Her eyes grew wide. Was someone really going to come after her daddy with a machine gun? "That's a metaphor," Shrum told her. "What's a metaphor?" she asked.

Shrum was starting to explain when the girl's mother, Elizabeth Edwards, stepped in and said firmly, "There's not going to be a machine gun in the debate."

Edwards's marching orders for the debate were: "Go get him." The former trial lawyer was forceful but measured, saying to Cheney, "You are still not being straight with the American people." Edwards had practiced saying, "You're lying to the American people," but the words sounded too blunt in rehearsal. In the debate, Cheney was a little grumpy but not as harsh as he routinely appeared to be on the campaign trail. The debate was essentially a draw; it did not move the numbers either one way or the other.

Before the first debate in Miami, Bush staffers had stood around with reporters joking about Kerry's odd skin color. (Kerry seemed to have put on a fake tan, which was gone by the time he took the stage against Bush.) After the Miami debate the mocking tone was gone. At Bush rallies, Rove and Hughes could be seen staring intently at the crowds, measuring reactions, taking notes. The news climate suddenly seemed to be turning against the president. Bush's former proconsul in Baghdad, Paul Bremer, was quoted as saying that he had futilely urged the president to send more troops to Iraq (accosted by angry Bush aides, Bremer meekly protested that his remarks had been off the record). The CIA issued a final report on WMD in Iraq. Rove was furious, as usual, at the press coverage. The "pro-Kerry *New York Times*," he fumed, played up the CIA's finding that Saddam had destroyed his WMD stockpiles. Buried by the "liberal press" was the finding that Saddam had been playing cat and mouse, hoping to lull the United Nations into dropping oil sanctions on Iraq so he could start building up his WMD arsenal again.

Then there was the annoying buzz over the mysterious lump on Bush's back during the first debate. Some viewers thought they had observed an odd bulge in the president's suit coat when the cameras viewed him from behind. The Internet lit up with conspiracy theories. The bulge was actually a box, suggested some bloggers—a transmitter that would allow Bush's aides to coach him while he groped for answers. The proof was flimsy or speculative, and the White House firmly denied that Bush had anything unusual affixed to his back. But they had to produce the president's tailor to take the fall for allowing Bush's suit coat to "pucker" when he leaned forward. The back-and-forth just dredged up old jokes about Bush as Junior, the puppet president, and undercut his hard-won standing as a war leader.

The answer to Bush's predicament, Rove & Co. believed, was to hit harder at Kerry. In attacking his opponent, Bush began quoting boxer Joe Louis: "He can run, but he can't hide," a line he had normally reserved for terrorists. It is risky to sharply attack an opponent toward the end of a campaign, according to conventional political wisdom. Negative campaigning by the incumbent can drive down his approval rating, and Bush's was already precariously hovering around 50 percent. But his handlers figured that he was a known commodity, and that voters weren't going to change their minds about him at this stage. The key was to do everything possible to destroy Kerry.

Bush was loaded for bear when he stepped onto the stage at Washington University in St. Louis for the town meeting on Oct. 8. His handlers were nervous: one of his advisers forlornly predicted that if the president blew this one, the election was lost. Just before the debate, he had insisted on being left alone for 15 minutes—unusual for a man who likes to be surrounded by company. Gone was the dismissive air of "Why am I here? Do I really have to debate this guy?" After watching a tape of his snarly Debate One performance, Bush had hammed it up at debate prep, putting on exaggerated scowls. But he had worked hard, practicing for hours before an "audience" that included national-security adviser Condoleezza Rice. (His sparring partner, Judd Gregg, had been called before 7 A.M. the day after the Miami debate and warned not to make any plans for the weekend.) Bush's handlers hoped that their man would feed off audience response. He does better when he is relating to people (other than surly reporters at a press conference). In Miami he had been staring into a vast, dark hall; the audience had been forbidden to clap or laugh.

The questioners at the St. Louis town meeting were just a few feet away, arrayed in a semicircle around the candidates. Bush winked and japed and chuckled ("heh, heh"). For the most part, the audience just stared back in stony silence. The citizens, "soft" Kerry and "soft" Bush voters selected by the Gallup polling organization, had been preparing questions and listening to instructions all day long in the chilly auditorium. They seemed stunned into somnolence by the seriousness of their responsibility on national TV.

Bush did not have a great night, but he did not have a bad one, either, and his handlers decided to put on a little victory dance to gin up momentum in Spin Alley. A half hour before the debate ended, they began appearing amid the reporters, high-fiving each other. The debate was in the bag! Or so they pretended. They actually believed Bush had eked out a tie, which was by and large the verdict of the press corps, though the overnight polls seemed to credit Kerry with another win.

Kerry's team thought their man had won round two as well. He was cool and calm, presidential enough, though there was something slightly mechanical about his performance. Alessandra Stanley, the TV reporter for *The New York Times,* noted that Kerry at moments looked like a flight attendant giving instructions on how to open the emergency exit. His handlers were relieved that their man had carried a microphone for the town meeting. It stopped him from making so many hand gestures.

K ERRY WAS BACK IN THE RACE. One more debate win, and he could ride the momentum to victory on Election Day. Remarkably, history seemed to be repeating itself: Comeback Kerry, finishing strong, confounding the odds-makers who had counted him out. Kerry felt anything but relaxed and confident, however, on the morning of the third debate, on Oct. 13 in Tempe, Ariz. He was irritated by a headline in a Santa Fe, N.M., newspaper, TIME TO BREAK THE TIE. Kerry was tense and whiny: "I don't understand this," he groused to an aide. "I've beaten the guy twice now—and somehow it's a tie. Why is this a must-win for me? When is it going to be a must-win for him?"

For all their bluster and spin, Bush's advisers were very worried for their man. The format was the same as in the first debate, and the topic—domestic affairs—was not the president's strong suit. Bush was given some stylistic pointers: don't slump against the podium when you talk. Leaning in might work when you're getting cozy with a small crowd, he was warned, but on TV it's a disaster. Curiously, Bush got more positive feed-back from an old foe—Sen. John McCain. The two men may have loathed each other at the South Carolina primary in 2000, but at dinner the night before the Tempe debate, McCain was joking and laughing with the president, giving him a lift at a critical moment.

SMILING OFTEN, standing straight, the president was a stark contrast to the hunched and scowling Bush of the first debate. Still, the transformation was perhaps a little too obvious. Some aides worried that Bush had repeated the mistake of Gore in 2000—Bush's opponent in those debates had been too hot in the first debate, too cold in the second and, as the guileless Gore himself had put it, "just right" in the third. Throughout the three debates, Bush and Kerry had seemingly reversed roles, with Kerry seeming calm and in charge while Bush played the role of challenger, nipping at his heels. The imagery was all wrong: the president was supposed to be the steady one, not changing personas from debate to debate.

Kerry was sure he had won the final debate. When the debate team came onto the plane afterward, Kerry, all smiles, hugged Shrum hard and said, "Thanks." Shrum felt redeemed. He hadn't felt so much affection from Kerry since the night they had won the Iowa caucuses back in January.

But in a conference room a few minutes away from the auditorium of Arizona State University, Republican pollster Ed Goeas knew better. About 30 minutes into the debate, Kerry was asked by moderator Bob Schieffer of CBS whether he thought homosexuality was a matter of choice or birth. In his answer, Kerry brought up Dick Cheney's gay daughter, Mary. Goeas's focus group—five Republicans, five Democrats, five independents—had a "huge negative reaction," Goeas later recalled. The group seemed to react differently to Kerry after his remark about Mary. Their comments, recorded on notecards after the Democratic candidate answered each question, became more wary and suspicious: "He didn't answer the question" or "He answered the question with an attack on the president." When the debate was over, 11 of the 15 cast votes for Bush.

Watching the debate in a trailer crammed with more than 20 advisers and staffers, Karl Rove knew right away that Kerry had blundered. He was sure Kerry had made the remark deliberately, using the term "lesbian" rather than the more benign "gay" to describe the vice president's daughter. Rove figured that Kerry was trying to shock the Christian right, Bush's base, into staying home on Election Day. Rove was exultant: Good, he thought. This tells voters that Kerry is who you thought he was, a cheesy pol who would say anything to get elected.

Kerry's remark was a break for the Bush campaign. The flap over the Mary Cheney remark diverted attention from Bush's performance and put the spotlight squarely on Kerry. Mary Beth Cahill did not help matters by saying after the debate that Mary was "fair game" (the veep's daughter was, in fact, long out of the closet, a gay activist herself). Kerry's aides insisted that the candidate's remark had not been intentional, that he was just trying to say something nice about Mary but sounded "klutzy" instead. (Indeed, both Tad Devine and Shrum had grimaced when they heard Kerry make the remark as they nervously watched the debate from their trailer.)

The explanations were too late. So-called security moms who had been initially inclined to vote for Bush, then swung toward Kerry after the first two debates, were put off by his seemingly gratuitous attempt to drag Cheney's daughter into the race. Kerry's momentum was stopped. With less than three weeks to go, both sides were claiming narrow leads. The race looked dead even.

EIGHT

The Endgame:
Down to the Wire

In the last weeks, Rove felt "emotional stress"
about getting out the vote for Bush.
And where was the "Comeback Kerry"
of campaign legend?

K ARL ROVE CULTIVATED AN AIR of mystery, rarely
appearing on TV talk shows or giving on-the-
record interviews. He wasn't all that elusive—he
sent e-mails by the score from his ubiquitous BlackBerry.
But he enjoyed taunting reporters. After Elisabeth Bumiller
of *The New York Times* wrote that the "normally elusive"
Rove was out spinning reporters after the first debate, Rove
declared to a press gaggle, "I must go. I must be elusive."
Rove was amused by the Internet rumor mill's suggestion
that the mysterious bulge on Bush's back at the first debate
was actually a secret transmitter. Spotting some reporters at
a Bush speech, he went into a pantomime of Rove the

Machiavellian Puppet Master, cupping his hand over his mouth and pretending to dictate the president's speech through a hidden microphone.

Jolly Karl. Actually, he was feeling a good deal of "emotional stress," as he somewhat stiffly put it to a *Newsweek* reporter. He was two weeks away from finding out whether his get-out-the-vote machine, so carefully and laboriously constructed during the past four years, was the crowning glory of King Karl—or a house of cards. Rove had been caught by surprise in 2000 when a seemingly solid win—a "landslide," Rove had predicted to the then Gov. George W. Bush two days before the election—turned into a popular-vote loss and the messy drama of hanging chads in Florida. In 2000 some 4 million Christian evangelicals—Rove's true believers—had stayed home on Election Day, put off by last-minute publicity over an old DUI conviction of George Bush and a general distaste for politics. Just as galling, the Democrats' get-out-the-vote operation had been arguably more effective than Rove's. The Democrats were really pouring it on this time around, using more than $100 million generated by 527s and Big Labor to register hundreds of thousands of new voters. Somewhat ominously, the Democrats were also creating a vast network of lawyers to file legal challenges on election night.

Rove was determined to fight back, even to strike preemptively. "They hired 10,000 lawyers. So we hired 10,000 lawyers," he said. Rove had already ordered up legal challenges to allegedly fraudulent Democratic voter-registration efforts in states from Ohio to Nevada. ("We found Freddy

The return of Bubba: Clinton was Kerry's October surprise

(Photo by Khue Bui for *Newsweek*)

Krueger [from the movie *Nightmare on Elm Street*] registered 10 times in Nevada," said an aide to Rove.) The Democrats hired poll watchers and drivers to get their people to the polling place. Traditionally, the Democrats could count on labor unions to organize the most effective get-out-the-vote operations. The Republicans, by custom, relied largely on volunteers, housewives and grandmothers, small business- men and retirees, who worked for nothing more than an "at- tawaytogo" message from Rove's BlackBerry and the satisfaction of playing a small part in his vast crusade to re- elect the president.

Volunteers or no (and lately, Rove had been hiring some get-out-the-vote professionals, as well as squadrons of lawyers), he wanted to maintain absolute control. He was obsessed with "metrics," with precise measurements of how the Bush-Cheney campaign was doing at any given mo- ment. "Give me a date," Rove demanded of a *Newsweek* reporter in mid-October. "Sept. 30?" He tapped into his com- puter to examine one of his "metric mileposts." "In Ohio we were supposed to register 1,119 voters that day. We registered 3,604!" he declared triumphantly.

Rove was feeling a little cranky about press reports that the Democrats were registering vastly more voters in swing states like Ohio and Florida. He blamed shoddy reporting by *The New York Times* (Rove considered the *Times* to be *Pravda* for liberals; he had just personally chewed out the *Times*'s ex- ecutive editor Bill Keller and Washington bureau chief Phil Taubman). The *Times* had measured only recent registration numbers, overlooking the fact, Rove protested, that the

GOP had been working away at voter registration since the 2000 election. "Nationally, it's a wash," claimed Rove. Besides, the key to victory was not registration, but turnout—actually getting people to the polls. Rove scorned a story in that morning's *Washington Post* reporting that Rove had given up a more ambitious effort to reach out to swing voters in order to concentrate on mobilizing the Republican base. "Ridiculous," he said. "We need 51 percent, and the base is only the high 30s." Rove, who studies population-migration tracts the way baseball fans study box scores, said he was particularly focused on finding and securing the "ex-urban vote," city dwellers and suburbanites who had just arrived in new towns and had been too busy getting settled to register to vote. These were the real "persuadables," the key to the election. ("Carver County, Minn. Fifty percent population increase. We got 62 percent there last time," said Rove, spouting factoids while he thumbed his BlackBerry.)

EVEN GREATER TORRENTS of statistics flowed from the mouth of Ken Mehlman, the BC04 campaign manager who oversaw the Republicans' ground game. President Bush had paid Mehlman his highest compliment one afternoon after the 2002 elections, as the president and his top political advisers sat around at Camp David watching football on TV. "He's a good general," President Bush said, nodding at Mehlman. "He's about to have a huge army." Mehlman was a familiar type in campaigns, only more so. In *The Making of the President 1960,* Theodore H. White described the "overdeveloped organizational sense" of certain Republican moneymen in the Nixon campaign. Mehlman loved organizing; his aides suspected that he made lists from lists. His aides once tortured him by taking away his BlackBerry in a restaurant. Sweating (so the story goes), Mehlman ended up ordering his assistant to read him his text messages out loud.

To enforce the strict, top-down command structure on the volunteer army in the field, Mehlman's top two deputies, political director Terry Nelson and field director Coddy Johnson, held a 10-hour teleconference with state and local operatives every Saturday. Working from a sheet of metrics, Johnson and Nelson would demand to know: How many calls were made, how many doorbells rung? Were the voter contacts personal or pamphlet drops? Johnson read books like *Seven Habits of Highly Effective People* and *The Tipping Point*. He played good cop: "All right, you guys are doing it! We're gonna make it! We're only 30 percent but we're gonna get there!" Nelson, also known as the Hammer, played bad cop. Johnson liked to imitate Nelson's growling at the state coordinators in a flat Iowa baritone: "I'm very concerned that you all stink. And have not made any progress."

The get-out-the-vote operation was all very organized and disciplined, but would it work on Election Day? In his Houston law office, Pat Oxford, 62, coordinator of a roughly 1,500-member GOP volunteer organization grandly known as the Mighty Texas Strike Force, just laughed. "They think you can send out lightning bolts from Washington, D.C.," said Oxford, whose 10-man teams could be parachuted into swing states to help fill gaps as campaign workers. "Young people think that you can plug it into a computer and it all comes out the same way." He described every Election Day as chaotic, or, as he put it in cattleman's lingo, "a calf scramble." ("This is not my first rodeo," said Oxford, who has worked in Bush campaigns since George H.W. Bush ran for the U.S. Senate in 1970.) Volunteers didn't always show up. A group of Strike Force volunteers from Dallas dispatched to the Midwest had just announced they had to go home two days before the election in order to trick or treat with their kids on Halloween. Oxford's teams ("We move to the sound of the guns") were originally coordinated by a young woman at RNC headquarters in Washington. "Wonderful young girl," said Oxford. One day a few weeks before Election Day, she stopped returning phone calls. Oxford imagined her overwhelmed by the pressure, "under her desk," he said, chuckling, "in a fetal position, sucking her thumb."

No wonder Karl Rove believed that he had to be hands-on, that he had to meet face to face with local organizers at campaign stops as he traveled with the president. As Election Day drew nearer, he was not in Washington planning grand strategy but in small Midwestern towns discussing canvassing operations in minute detail with his eager but untested volunteers. On these trips, he could pretend to be the merry prankster, throwing snowballs at reporters in Wisconsin, but he missed home. For all his playacting as master of the political universe, Rove is a family man often seen at his son's school events. He dislikes overnight travel. "It's a good thing," he said, "that 80 percent of the persuadables live east of the Mississippi." He was speaking metrically. In other words, he could take day trips and still make it home some nights to see his family.

In Reno, Nev., as the campaign entered the final week, John Kerry was given a hero's welcome. A crowd of nearly 20,000 packed into an arena at the University of Nevada and rose to their feet as one at the mention of Kerry's name. They did not sit back down again. When the applause finally subsided, Kerry launched into a long and rambling speech, one of his most soporific in weeks. A simple line in his prepared text on the need to fix Social Security became a five-minute explanation of how the system got broken. He gave the same prolix treatment to health care, with a strange overreaching assertion that the Bush health-care plan was "killing millions of Americans." A 25-minute speech went on for close to an hour.

Kerry knew that he had regressed. Walking off the stage, he turned to his daughter Vanessa and said, "I went too long, didn't I?" Vanessa just nodded. She was trying not to criticize too much. Sometimes she would say, "Love ya, dude, but that was too long." Her sister, Alex, the film director, would tell her father, "You have your audience for 20 minutes, and once you hit the climax of that speech you're never going to be able to go that high again. You've got to come down because you need to leave them wanting more." Her father would improve, for a little while.

Vanessa would force herself to laugh at the old jokes and cheer heartily as she stood onstage with her father. Alex made less of an effort. Since June she had been making a film about her experiences on the trail and whenever her father started droning on too long she would unceremoniously exit the stage, claiming that she "had to go shoot." Teresa was no longer onstage. She had always said that she did not wish to be the candidate's wife, staring up adoringly at her man. After her trying time on the Sea to Shining Sea tour, the handlers decided she was better off campaigning alone. It was up to the girls to play the humanizing presence at their father's side.

The energy was back in the Kerry campaign after the debates, but it wasn't back in the candidate. Vanessa was heartened that the crowds were huge and wildly enthusiastic even if her father did wander on. Maybe something big was starting to happen. But where was Kerry the comeback man? The candidate and his family had the answer: "Comeback Kerry" was a fiction, a myth propagated by the press in need of a good story and promoted by the campaign. The family never talked about it. "I don't really think Dad sees it," said Alex. Still, the candidate was perfectly happy to play along. At the Reno rally, Sen. Harry Reid told the audience that John Sasso had assured him that "John Kerry always fights hardest in the final moments of a campaign." The crowd cheered loudly. Onstage, Kerry smiled and nodded along.

Kerry's daughters were surprised and upset at how nasty and personal the Bushes and Cheneys were willing to get. The girls had no love for the opposition themselves. Though Alex and Vanessa never openly criticized the president, their faces would fill with rage when they heard him discuss the most mundane subjects. Watching Bush debate her father,

Alex was struck by what she described as the "strange . . . surreal darkness that exists" in the president. Alex was having a cheerful breakfast with her father in his Las Vegas hotel room the day after the last debate. As she was eating, she heard some staffers chattering about the burgeoning controversy over Kerry's remark about Mary Cheney. The frenzy seemed absurd to her and, she thought, to her father as well. After breakfast, she flipped on the morning news to see a scowling Lynne Cheney calling Kerry's remarks "a cheap and tawdry political trick" and describing her father as "not a good man." This seemed like a new low to her. She vowed if she ever met "that woman" she would not shake her hand.

Traditionally, campaigns end on an up note. The race may have been a slog through a swamp, but the candidate is supposed to exit on the high road. Told to create a heart-tugging final campaign ad, Fred Davis, the Bush adman based in California, cut a spot entitled "It Is Time," a collage of gauzy images of Bush meeting with soldiers, of firefighters looking resolute amid the devastation of 9/11. But in the end, the race was too close and too brutish for the high-road treatment. Kerry spent most of the last week taking potshots at Bush after a *New York Times*/CBS investigation reported that 380 tons of high explosives—perfect for terrorist bombs—had mysteriously disappeared from an Iraqi bunker after the invasion. Kerry called the president "incompetent." So the Bush team decided it was necessary to bash Kerry one last time as weak and feckless.

T HE FINAL SWIPE was a fitting end to the most negative and most expensive air wars in political history. The candidates and the interest groups spent more than $1 billion (versus $100 million in 1996). By the last week, the two campaigns were burning money at the rate of $10 million a day. For almost a year, BC04 advertising chieftain Mark McKinnon had been looking for a good way to scare the American people, tastefully and subtly, of course. Almost a year earlier, the ad team had put together a spot called "Flame." The image was just a simple burning match, with a voice-over intoning, "There's a fire across the sea. And the flames of this fire have crossed oceans." The ad didn't test very well, and at any rate it was too high-concept for Karl Rove. McKinnon dusted off an old cold-war favorite, made by the Ronald Reagan campaign in the 1980s to scare Americans about the communist threat, called "The Bear in the Woods." Only this time the ad makers substituted wolves. A feathery-voiced woman warned that weakness always invited predators, while on the screen some wolves milled about a clearing, then started walking toward the camera. The feel was slightly reminiscent of *The Blair Witch Project*— unintended, according to McKinnon. But when some complained that the wolves looked more like German shepherds, McKinnon maintained that the Bush team had not wanted the beasts to look too vicious. Rove was persuaded to give the impressionistic ad a try. "OK, very arty, guys," said Rove, "but let's make sure it works."

McKinnon was strung out. He had a cold and joked that

he had a persistent ringing in his ears, possibly from his sinuses, possibly from the sheer noise generated by the campaign. The small, tight circle around Bush was hanging on, missing their families, wanting it to be over. Karen Hughes was sad because she couldn't be home with her son, a high-school senior applying early to Stanford. Communications Director Dan Bartlett had already sent his wife and young children to be with her parents in Houston; there was no point in keeping them in Washington because he was so rarely home. Matt Dowd, the self-avowed pessimist, had avoided the last debate; he was just too nervous. At a lunch with reporters with a week to go, he pretended, with a notable lack of conviction, to be optimistic about the race and finally explained, "I'm Irish: I worry about everything."

THE BUSHIES' COUNTERPARTS on the Kerry plane were just as exhausted, but at least one of them was feeling a lot happier than he had been before Labor Day. Reporters listening to Kerry make a speech in Orlando, Fla., on the last weekend noticed something very familiar. They had heard the phrases and cadences before in Kerry's speeches, but also in Al Gore's and Ted Kennedy's. It was classic Bob Shrum: the people versus the powerful. "America deserves a president who will fight for you and not only the people at the top," intoned Kerry. Shrum was back in the center of things, leaning over speechwriter Josh Gottheimer (Shrum can't type) at the word processor. The campaign was putting Shrum out on the Sunday talk shows. When he said he was too tired from his early-morning performance to attend a rally in Tampa on Sunday night, Kerry offered him his bed in the cabin of his campaign jet. Shrum slept for an hour and a half. "You missed a hell of a rally," Kerry told him. What was so great about it? asked Shrum. "I was pretty brief," said Kerry.

Osama bin Laden had given the Kerry campaign a good scare on Friday night. The tape of the Qaeda leader, creepily invoking polemical filmmaker Michael Moore, was played in the war room at Kerry headquarters in Washington. Pollster Mark Mellman noticed the quiet in the room and the color draining from people's faces. Was this the October Surprise? Was bin Laden going to get Bush re-elected by showing his fright mask on election eve?

Mellman saw a slight wobble in Kerry's polls overnight. He walked 45 minutes from his Georgetown home to headquarters downtown (he doesn't drive on the Sabbath) to present the potentially ominous results, but by Sunday Kerry had recovered. Perhaps voters had been numbed by the years of scratchy tapes smuggled out of Pakistan and the elevated threat levels. "Saturday Night Live" took out some of the sting by parodying the tape. In any case, by Sunday night the Kerry campaign was allowing itself to feel optimistic.

Kerry's last job on the last day of the campaign was basically to show up. There were no more strategic decisions to be made, no more staff squabbles to referee, no cell-phone calls to his ever-widening circle of advisers to make doubly sure he was making the right decision. And yet somehow Kerry was 45 minutes late to his first rally, scheduled to begin at 9:30 A.M. in Orlando. Kerry and Bush have opposite rhythms. Bush loves the mornings and feeds off crowds but tires noticeably as the day drags on. For Kerry, morning is not his best time, and he rarely seems to get a lift from the crowd—but he has a kind of dogged stamina. On this morning, the last of the campaign, President Bush had begun with a rally in Ohio at 7:30. Air Force One was taking off from Milwaukee airport (Bush's third event) just as Kerry was arriving there for his first major event of the day. The press corps just assumed that Kerry was late because he was on the phone, but they wondered: Whom did he really have to talk to at this point? What was there left to say?

And yet, when Kerry did take the stage, he was compelling. He was crisp and sharp, all the things he had never managed to be in the campaign. Later that night at Joe Louis Arena in Detroit, Kerry brought out an old line to get back at Bush. Citing Bush's "You can run but you can't hide" line, Kerry reminded the audience of Muhammad Ali's taunt to George Foreman: "George, is that all you got?" The crowd loved it.

At 9 P.M. in Cleveland, Kerry was introduced by Bruce Springsteen (referred to at an earlier rally by Kerry as "a sort of minstrel poet, if you will"). Teresa was at last reunited with her husband. Shielding her eyes from the klieg lights she hated, she spoke softly into the mike, but she, too, rose to the occasion with brief, gracious remarks. By this time Kerry was basking and beaming.

Kerry's sharpness did not come as a complete surprise to Alex. She thought that her father was addicted to focus. She didn't think he suffered from adult attention-deficit disorder, but she knew that he was better off free from distractions. She remembered that during a run-through before the second debate—his weakest performance—he had behaved like a little boy who refused to do his homework, teasingly throwing things at his daughter as his aides vainly tried to give him comments. Tonight Kerry had nothing left to do but show up and smile for the cameras.

The mood on Air Force One on the last weekend was upbeat—by decree. Karen Hughes was determined to show the president as cheerful, happy, joking, no matter what. Aides told reporters that the president was cracking jokes and wearing a funny shirt that said BOWLING FOR BUSH. Hughes herself reported that the president had told her, "Do you think Kerry's having this much fun?" His aides made a show of clowning around. Rove somewhere found a sign that said FREE KITTENS, and hung it in the conference room of Air Force One. On Halloween, top advisers dressed up in camouflage jackets—to mock Kerry, who had worn camo to stage a duck-hunting photo op in Ohio. The president was reportedly playing a happy-go-lucky game of gin rummy, complete with a referee (deputy chief of staff Joe Hagin) to wave a yellow flag in case anyone got out of hand.

But when the president showed up to vote at 7:30 on election morning at the Crawford, Texas, firehouse, his eyes seemed puffy and he looked worn. The final rally the night before at Southern Methodist University had been lackluster and hurried. Bush's cockiness was gone. "We'll see how it goes tonight," Bush told reporters. "I've given it my all . . .

I've enjoyed it." He thanked his old nemesis, the White House press corps, for its coverage. Laura Bush's smile was plastered on her face. She took her husband's hand and intensely kneaded it with her thumb.

The tracking polls overnight in Florida showed the race looking tight. But as they flew back to Washington, Bush told his top advisers that he had spoken to brother Jeb, the governor of the all-important swing state. Jeb was a straight talker, said the president, and Jeb felt good about his state. Bush seemed confident enough, thought McKinnon.

But McKinnon's own mood darkened when he arrived at the Bush-Cheney campaign headquarters in Arlington shortly after 5 P.M. In Pit Row, strategy boss Dowd was in his office with the door shut. McKinnon tucked his head in. Dowd looked serious, even a little exasperated. His phone was ringing constantly and e-mails were stacking up on his computer screen. Dowd was puzzled by the network exit polls. They were grim: Bush was getting crushed in Pennsylvania and losing in Ohio and Florida. But something was odd. The polls were based on a turnout of 59 percent women and 41 percent men. Maybe that was the actual turnout, but Dowd doubted it. Also, Bush seemed to be doing surprisingly well with Hispanics, winning 42 percent of their votes. But if that number was true, then Bush should be cleaning up overall. The numbers didn't seem to make sense.

The rest of Bush's media team was supposed to be celebrating at a pub called Ireland's Four Courts Restaurant and Bar across the street from Bush-Cheney headquarters. When ad man Fred Davis showed up at 6 P.M., the place was a morgue. He ran into another team member, Russ Schriefer, who asked, "What did we do wrong?" The two men unhappily headed back to the office. The mood was silent, down. People were dejectedly looking down at their computers. Davis wondered into Dowd's office. The strategy guru was still wound-up and grumpy, but he was starting to unravel the mystery. The exit polls were flawed, Dowd announced. He allowed himself, for once, to be an optimist. We're going to win, he predicted. It was just that no one knew it yet.

ACROSS THE POTOMAC, at Kerry headquarters, Michael Whouley, the mastermind of Kerry's Iowa victory, was doing everything he could to get out the vote. There had been reports of massive turnout—good news for Kerry, who was counting on new voters to put him over the top. Whouley was standing in the middle of something called the Bullseye Room, snapping off decisions large and small. In Cleveland, people who had been waiting in line for hours were complaining about the lack of restrooms. An aide to Whouley dispatched Porta Pottis. More complex complaints were referred to the Breakdown Room. In Philadelphia, there was a report that when a computerized voting machine was switched on that morning, it showed 400 votes already recorded. Lawyers were dispatched; the report turned out to be a rumor. Headquarters was crawling with lawyers, most of them with nothing to do. They were dressed in jeans, not suits. "We're trying to hide," said one.

Shortly before 9 P.M., at the Republican National Committee headquarters up on Capitol Hill, the RNC's top oppo man, Tim Griffin, was feeling reborn. With Johnny Cash's "Ring of Fire" playing, Griffin was watching four TV sets and realizing that the early-afternoon exit polls had been just plain wrong. "We're up in Michigan!" he exclaimed. "We're gonna win Florida and we're gonna win Ohio! If we win Florida and Ohio, game over!" After a very blue afternoon, he was feeling exultant. "The exit polls stink. I could throw a dart at a map and get a better number." About an hour later, back in Arlington, McKinnon was feeling the same sense of reprieve. "Back from the death swoon," he said. "The projections were completely wrong. It's just unbelievable." McKinnon was watching the electoral map. "It looks like it's all coming down to Ohio," he said. "We're planning to have a ritual burning of the exit polls."

At the White House, Karl Rove had set up quarters in the family dining room. (He had joked to reporters that he would be working in the "bat cave.") National-security adviser Condoleezza Rice wandered in and out and joked that Rove was looking at way too many numbers. Rove was studying comparisons of results in Florida and Ohio with the poll data in the 2000 election. At about 10:30, he called over to the senior staff, nervously hovering around the Roosevelt Room, and told them that the president would win both Florida and Ohio. The cheers were so loud that they could be heard down the hall in the press briefing room. Then ABC News called Florida for Bush; another eruption. Only now did Karen Hughes finally admit that the White

House had drafted two speeches—one for a concession. It no longer looked that the second speech would be necessary.

In Copley Square in Boston, the fans had stopped chanting, "We want a party!" The Red Sox Nation euphoria was dissipating along with Senator Kerry's chances. The ballroom of the Fairmont Copley Plaza suddenly felt like a ghost town. All the top Kerry aides, on hand to spin reporters, suddenly vanished. The buffet table was deserted. A few junior aides hung around.

At the White House, the Secret Service was told to prepare a motorcade to go over to the Ronald Reagan Building, where the party faithful were awaiting the president's victory speech. But there was a nagging glitch: the networks were refusing to declare any more states for Bush. His electoral tally, according to NBC and Fox, stood at 269, one shy of the 270 necessary to win. The Kerry campaign put out a defiant statement, refusing to concede anything. Bush was frustrated. He wanted to claim the victory he knew to be his. But Rove counseled caution. They had to wait. A long night was getting longer.

For the Kerry camp, reality began to set in around 9 P.M., when the Democrats realized that Bush would take Florida after all. The news was not entirely a surprise. Despite some giddiness over the exit polls earlier in the day, Kerry's own experts knew the numbers might be misleading. Kerry's polls had turned south overnight on Monday. Still, the Kerry-ites clung to one last hope, that Ohio might still fall into the Democratic column. When NBC and Fox called Ohio for Bush around 1 A.M., Kerry's advisers eyed a last-ditch strategy—holding out for a late count that would include "provisional votes" that would not be counted for another 10 days.

But the numbers did not add up. The number of provisional votes hovered around Bush's margin of victory in Ohio, and the campaign recognized that only a portion of them came from pro-Kerry counties. Nothing but a miracle could save Kerry, and the candidate and his advisers saw that the long wait and inevitable court fights would paint Kerry as a sore loser. Adviser Ron Klain presented an aggressive legal strategy, but Kerry decided to spare the country.

Just after 11 A.M., Kerry called the president and conceded. The conversation between the two old enemies was gracious. "I hope you are proud of the effort you put in," Bush told Kerry. Both men agreed that the country had grown too divided, that both sides need to reach out.

Shortly after 2 P.M., Kerry took the stage in historic Faneuil Hall in Boston. In a raspy voice, he spoke about "the danger of division and the need, the desperate need, for unity, for common ground, for coming together." Kerry showed an unusual flash of emotion, his voice catching as he thanked his friends and family from his heart. Less than an hour later, President Bush struck the same themes of unity and common purpose at a rally near the White House.

If those two men could forgive each other, maybe Americans separated by the great Red-Blue divide can do the same.

NINE

Campaign 2008:
Now What?

Kerry wonders what went wrong,
while Bush declares a mandate.
But will he succumb to the second-term curse?

ON THURSDAY, NOVEMBER 11, nine days after the election, John Kerry asked a *Newsweek* reporter to come to his house on Louisburg Square in Boston. Kerry opened the door and led the guest into a book-lined living room. With oriental rugs, red lacquered walls and a giant ship model, the room was fit for a merchant prince. Just up Beacon Hill, Kerry's ancestor, John Winthrop, had delivered his "shining city on a hill" sermon almost four centuries ago.

Kerry looked like he had not slept in about two years, but his mood seemed chipper, or at least resolute. "I'm not going to go lick my wounds or hide under a rock or disappear. I'm going to learn. I've had disappointments and I've learned to cope. I've lost friends, a marriage, I've lost things in life," he said. He was critical of *Newsweek*'s election narrative as gossipy and unduly harsh on him, his wife and his campaign staff. For two hours, holding the election issue of the magazine in his hand, he discussed the campaign, from time to time seeking to correct what he regarded as factual inaccuracies or distortions of the truth.

He said that he bore no animus toward George Bush. The two men had different "world views," he said. There were "those of us who felt called by the Kennedy years to change the world versus the people who were indifferent—for whom it meant nothing." He said he was proud of his effort, and that he had nearly overcome President Bush's enormous advantages of incumbency and his three-year head start at identifying and getting out voters. No one had ever defeated a sitting war president, he said, but he had come pretty close. (FDR and Lincoln were re-elected during wars; Truman and LBJ chose not to run again.) Kerry said that he had been a good communicator and connected with voters, but he did not wish to be quoted saying so. He did not want to appear boastful or defensive.

He rejected the portrayal of him as a loner who had no real confidantes on the campaign plane. "I have a bunch of them," he said, mentioning David Thorne and Boston political consultant John Martilla, among others. "But I didn't ask them to travel until the end because they were doing other things in the campaign. Most of these people have been in my political life for 35 years. I don't tire of people who give me good advice." He defended Mary Beth Cahill, his campaign

Hubris?: "I earned capital in the campaign, and I intend to spend it," said the president, with Laura (Photo by Charles Ommanney/Contact for *Newsweek*)

manager: "She took a huge weight off of me. She liberated me to be the candidate." And he said that his cell phone had not been taken away from him; "I gave the phone to Sasso for a week," he said. Kerry offered several other corrections or clarifications that have been included in the preceding narrative.

Though Kerry bridled at times, his manner through most of the conversation was calm and good humored. He seemed to invite criticism. He said that he had learned a great deal from the campaign, and it was clear that he though he could improve his performance. He seemed particularly interested in finding a new form of political rhetoric, one that seemed less tired, formal and stilted. Perhaps, he surmised, there was a way to speak in a more natural and conversational style. He regretted that he had not found more ways to speak from the heart, that that he had waited until his concession speech to show palpable emotion. Kerry sounded very much like a man who was thinking of running again, though he protested, "it's way too soon."

As the reporter left and walked down the street away from the house, Kerry called out to him by name. He came down the sidewalk holding a letter that had just been left on his doorstep. It was written in the hand of a schoolgirl and read, in part, "John Kerry, you're the greatest!" Kerry looked directly into the reporter's eye, as if he was searching for something. "The pundits have never liked me," he said. "I don't know why. Is it the way I look? The way I sound?" His toothy smile returned, he shrugged and shook hands. It was the only time in the evening that he seemed genuinely per-plexed or vulnerable.

IMMEDIATELY AFTER THE ELECTION, Karl Rove told re-porters that this election was his last, that he would never again run a presidential campaign. Two weeks later, he was hedging a little in a conversation with a *Newsweek* reporter. "I was completely exhausted when I said that," Rove said. "I can't imagine doing it again, but maybe I would. There are not a lot of people who have done two of these things in their lives. It's the hardest thing I have ever done." Rove claimed that, despite all the advantages of incumbency, he had a harder time running this Bush campaign than the 2000 effort. The Rove machine had become a sprawling empire, with various far-flung fiefdoms that had to be tended to. While the Bush campaign may have looked like a highly cen-tralized juggernaut—with Rove in complete charge—actu-ally it required keeping "about 15 different camps happy," Rove said. "It didn't play to my skill sets. Stroking egos—I'm not good at that. I had to spend more time communicating with people so they couldn't say, 'I was blindsided.'" Rove says that the demands of the campaign tested his ties of friendship with President Bush. "There are only so many times you can say, 'Sir, that's bull s—. I know you're tired but you've got to go to Indiana one more time, you've got to get on that bus, you've got to travel three days in a row.' I was only able to do it because I had a thirty-year friendship."

Rove said that for all his troubles keeping his campaign on track, his job was easier than Kerry's. He had watched, intrigued and apalled, as the Kerry campaign stumbled through staff upheavals and the intervention of the Clintonistas. "The guy was isolated. It was hard enough for me to say, 'You've got to do this.' I can't imagine what it was like when you had few people you could really call your own," said Rove. He did not really sound all that gleeful about Kerry's woes. He almost sounded sympathetic.

To THE VICTOR BELONG THE SPOILS, or at least a moment of celebratory indulgence. On Saturday, November 13, Bush's national security adviser, Condoleezza Rice, thought she was going out to dinner with some family to celebrate her 50th birthday. Instead, her car delivered her to the British Embassy, an ornate imperial pile up above embassy row on Massachusetts Avenue. There the president of the United States and the First Lady, as well Karl Rove and Karen Hughes and about a hundred other members of the Bush Ascendancy, waited to toast her. The party was black tie, and Rice, who is known for her stylish dress, felt uncomfortably informal. But only briefly: she was escorted to a private room where she found her hair dresser standing at the ready and a red satin Oscar de la Renta dress laid out on the bed. Suitably coiffed and gowned, Rice floated down the marble stair case "like Cinderella," said a Bush family friend. Champagne flutes were lofted and drained. The president, drinking ginger ale, beamed like the proud father of a debutante.

Two days later, President Bush made Rice his Secretary of State.

Colin Powell was retiring, none too soon for the Bush loyalists who thought Powell was a little too open about his disagreements with administration hawks (Powell was particularly resented for his "I told you so" account of opposing the invasion of Iraq). When Powell suggested that he might stick around for a little longer to re-start the Middle East peace process, now that Yassir Arafat was gone, President Bush politely, but firmly, declined. Powell's outspoken wife, Alma, did not hide her feelings in private conversations with friends. Her husband had been treated "unconscionably" by the president and his team, she said. His departure meant the final triumph of Cheney-Rumsfeld hardliners, a prospect she found "scary."

It had never been clear where Rice had stood in the endless battles between Powell at State and Rumsfeld at Defense. Most foreign policy experts said (though rarely for quotation) that Rice had been too easily rolled, that she had done poorly at her job of coordinating between warring parties in the national security establishment. But it was obvious that Rice was close to the president, and that wherever she ended up on an issue was exactly where the president wanted her to be.

The president was consolidating his power. The Bush family circle was in charge. As Attorney General, John Ashcroft, apostle of the Religious Right, was replaced by Alberto Gonzales, the White House counsel, an old Bush friend from Texas widely regarded as just as malleable as Condi

Rice. At the CIA, the new director, former Republican Congressman Porter Goss, was busily purging bureaucrats and circulating a memo warning against leaks critical of the administration. Throughout the government, Texas loyalists were being seeded into top jobs. Policy in the second Bush term would be made and executed straight out of the White House. There would be no independent power bases in the Washington of Bush II.

The president had been jocular, not so much cocky as happily confident, when he appeared for his first press conference two days after the election. He seemed to relish teasing reporters, telling them that the "people had spoken" and now he was going to enforce a one-question rule, i.e., no more annoying follow-up questions from the nattering nabobs in the press room. He made ritual gestures towards unity and reaching out; possibly, he was sincere. But he served notice that he meant to stick to his agenda, and it appeared, from his words and his tone, that he would be just as unyielding as he had been in the first term. "I earned capital in the campaign, political capital, and I intend to spend it. It is my style," he said.

Gone was any trace of the First Debate Scowl or the smirk that sometimes creeps across his lips when he is feeling belligerent or cornered. He seemed liberated; he had broken his father's one-term jinx and won a second term. He had been "mis-underestimated" by his opponent and much of the big media one last time. Bush did not gloat; he seemed to want to show the kind of calm humility that comes from genuine vindication.

But was he feeling perhaps a little too secure? Bush seems to take a defiant pride in not dwelling on doubt or self-reflection. Once, when *Washington Post* reporter Bob Woodward asked how history would view his presidency, he answered: "History. We don't know. We'll all be dead."

History suggests that Bush will be lucky to avoid a serious let down, if not disaster, in his second term. In theory, second-term presidents can dare to be statesman. They cannot run again; they have no reason to horde their political capital. But the last century is littered with the dashed hopes of failed second-term presidents. Indeed, two of the last three second-term presidents (Nixon and Clinton) were impeached, and the third (Reagan) avoided impeachment in part because, as one of his former aides succinctly put it, "they thought he was senile." (Reagan's defense in the Iran-contra scandal was, in essence, that he could not recall authorizing illegal arm sales to Iran.)

The dominant theme of second-term flops is hubris, an ancient affliction that has been known to grip President Bush from time to time. In retrospect, there are always omens, though the president, like the hero of a Greek tragedy, cannot see them. The paradigmatic example may be Bill Clinton's triumphant return to the White House on November 6, 1996, the day after he trounced his Republican opponent, Sen. Bob Dole. At the rope line, Clinton stopped to give (or receive) a big welcome home hug from a then obscure former White House intern named Monica Lewinsky.

"When they are first elected, presidents tend to think they're king of the mountain," said Harvard professor David

Gergen, who served Nixon, Reagan and Clinton. "When you're re-elected you think you're master of the universe. You go off and do crazy, reckless things." Woodrow Wilson was so impressed with his accomplishments as a global statesman that he forgot that all politics is local; he was humiliated when the Treaty of Versailles, which he negotiated to make the world safe for democracy after World War I, was rejected by the U.S. Congress. FDR's second term turned to embarrassment when he tried to pack the U.S. Supreme Court with justices who would do his bidding (FDR was saved largely by the coming of World War II). Eisenhower lost 49 House seats and 15 Senate seats and was rendered irrelevant two years into his second term. Nixon won 49 of 50 states in 1972; he was in exile less than three years later.

Bush (like Nixon before his crash) may have historic opportunities for statesmanship. Arafat's death does open possibilities, however fraught. Bush has said he wants to get involved in reviving the Middle East peace process. He would go a long way towards overcoming his caricature as a cowboy or a Crusader in European and Arab eyes if he makes a real effort. But Bush's idea of negotiation during the first term was to take a position and not budge until the other side cried uncle. He will have to show more nimbleness and cleverness to solve the Rubik's Cube of the Palestinian question. (He could start by hiring as his envoy former Secretary of State James A. Baker, who possesses some of the subtle deal-making skills that Bush appears to lack).

Bush could also tackle the long dreaded issue of entitlement reform. There is an obvious fix that would rescue the

Social Security system from a rising tide of red ink—raise the retirement age to 70 and slightly increase payroll taxes on the wealthy. But every other president for the past two decades has shied away from the so-called third rail of politics, and Bush seems mostly interested in allowing future retirees to privately invest a portion of their payroll taxes—a reform that would cost billions before it saved any money. The president has also promised to simplify the tax code, but it may be significant that the chairman of the Senate Finance Committee, Sen. Charles Grassley of Iowa, shows a deep reluctance to get into the maddening business of tax reform. For every winner there must a loser, and corporations with threatened loopholes hire lobbyists that can turn the legislative process into a morass of competing special interests.

Events have a way upsetting ambitious agendas. If Iraq splits apart in a true civil war, if Iran forges ahead towards a nuclear bomb, if China lobs a missile over Taiwan, if North Korea's demented leadership does something mad, or if the terrorists strike an American city again, Bush could quickly find himself playing crisis manager, not visionary. Iran, in particular, could easily become a second-term Iraq, only worse. If Condi Rice joins the hawks in threatening military action, she will face a revolt of her own State Department bureaucracy. And with the American military pinned down in Iraq, it's not at all clear the Pentagon could mount a successful operation to take down the mullahs or eliminate their growing nuclear capability.

Even if the world remains relatively calm, Bush will not

have smooth sailing on Capitol Hill. With 55 senators, the Republicans are still 5 votes shy of the 60 they need to shut down filibusters. That could mean paralysis, certainly if Bush chooses anyone but a moderate centrist to fill one of the several Supreme Court seats that are likely to open. There is some talk of strong-arm tactics, like outlawing filibusters, but that could just permanently freeze the polarization on the Hill.

Much will depend on the political skills of the Republicans' Senate majority leader, Bill Frist of Tennessee. Frist has proved something of a disappointment to the Washington elites. When he first arrived in Washington in 1994 he seemed to be a well-spoken, smooth Princeton man, a good catch for a Georgetown dinner party. But after he became majority leader in 2002 he began sounding like a fire-breathing Baptist preacher. The chattering classes in Washington are grumbling that Frist is selling his soul to the Religious Right because he wants to run for president in 2008 and hopes to position himself to march at the head of Karl Rove's evangelical legions.

In truth, says a Republican close to Frist, the senator has always been pretty conservative on social issues like abortion and gay marriage. The Washington establishment has just not wanted to see it. The kind of politician who can rise above partisanship is becoming increasingly rare in the Red-Blue world of shouting talking heads. Republican moderates have become almost as scarce as Southern Democrats. (In the once "solid South," the Democrats now occupy only four of 22 Senate seats.) The country is gradually tilting to the right almost everywhere but the big cities. On November 2, Bush carried every single rural county in America.

The Democratic party, grumbles its most colorfully outspoken champion, James Carville, is becoming "an opposition party, and not a particularly effective one." To become the majority party again, the Democrats will have to overcome a widening culture gap. While Kerry did win almost 49 percent of the popular vote, there were two ominous developments for the Democrats. The percentage of Hispanics voting Republican rose from 35 percent in 2000 to 44 percent. The Democrats had been counting on Hispanics, the fastest-growing demographic group, to give them a long term majority. But cultural issues like abortion and gay marriage are driving Hispanics to the right. Likewise, the Democrats have depended on a gender gap: while Republicans win males (especially southern white males), the Democrats win women. But a slight majority of married women with children voted for Bush. The reason, says Carville, is that Bush was able to sell fearful mothers a simple story line. "Bush's narrative was: I'm going to protect you from the terrorists of Tikrit and the homos of Hollywood," says Carville.

The Democrats need to find a new way of talking to heartland voters. Perhaps John Kerry will find a way to sound less like a stiff New Englander and more like a regular guy. But one of Kerry's advisers says he's waiting for instructions on the future of the party from "the boss—and I don't mean Springsteen." He was referring to Bill Clinton, the only national Democrat capable of winning Red State voters in recent years.

Clinton's wife Hillary is already positioning herself. At an off-the-record dinner at the Brookings Institution in Washington shortly after the election, she made a forceful case that the Democrats are going to have to listen more closely to the cultural values of the heartland—the revulsion with Hollywood and the coarsening of pop culture. At the dinner, a few attendees noted that Hillary's accent was sounding more and more corn fed, that she seemed to be acting and talking more like the Goldwater-supporting Midwestern girl she once was and less and less like the feminist-activist Yale Law School grad she became.

The 2008 campaign had begun.

ACKNOWLEDGMENTS

In 1984, *Newsweek* first detached a team of reporters, writers and editors to spend more than a year working on a single book-length article chronicling the presidential election. Every four years since then, *Newsweek* has followed the same model: our reporters seek access to the inner workings of the campaigns of the leading candidates on the understanding that none of the information will be published until after the votes are cast on Election Day. The information is then woven into a narrative that seeks to tell the inside story of the race for the White House.

The principal writer on the first three projects (1984, 1988 and 1992) was Peter Goldman, for many years *Newsweek*'s peerless craftsman of lead stories (or, as they're known at the magazine, "violins," after the first violin in an orchestra). I took over as election project writer from Peter for the 1996 campaign, but I have been lucky to have him as my all-purpose wise man/morale officer running the reporting team. Peter also brought his expertise and contacts to covering the high rise and dramatic fall of the Howard Dean candidacy.

Eleanor Clift covered her first presidential campaign almost three decades ago—in 1976, when she followed Jimmy Carter to the White House. She knows and understands politics as well as anyone in journalism. It was her job to cover the upper echelons of the Kerry campaign, a task she accomplished with her usual skill, shrewdness and aplomb. Eleanor's sidekick covering the Democrats in the primaries was Suzanne Smalley, an able and aggressive young journalist who was able to get deep inside the Kerry campaign in the early going. When Suzanne left to take a job at *The Boston Globe,* Jonathan Darman took over and used his sensitivity and perceptiveness to develop sources close to and inside the Kerry family; Jonathan's sense of the "big picture" of the Kerry campaign was also invaluable to shaping the narrative. Covering the tightly controlled Bush campaign was difficult; campaign officials closely monitored interviews and cut off access from time to time. But by remaining calm, resourceful and amiably persistent, Kevin Peraino was able to find the true stories behind the story put out by the Bush-Cheney spinners. I benefitted as well from the observations and smart reporting of *Newsweek's* regular White House reporter, Tamara Lipper.

At *Newsweek,* I worked with my long-time colleague Alexis Gelber, a smart and steady editor who knows how to put together large, complex projects and has a good feel for the human drama of politics. It takes many skilled hands to put together a package of this size. As our researcher, we were lucky to have one of the best diggers who has ever worked at *Newsweek,* Holly Bailey. I have nothing but respect and thanks for our great photographers Charles Ommanney, Khue Bui and David Hume Kennerly and our art staff and photo department, especially Michelle Molloy and Alex Ha. Our able publicist, Ken Weine, and our good lawyer, Steve Fuzesi, offered their always valuable services.

At PublicAffairs, let me thank my old friend Peter Osnos, a great newsman, who enthusiastically embraced the idea of turning the article into a book. Peter has created an essential institution at PublicAffairs, and his staff is first-rate. My gratitude and admiration go to managing editor Robert Kimzey, publicist Jaime Leifer, marketing director Lisa Kaufman, art director Nina D'Amario and page designer Jane Raese.

Finally, my thanks to my top editors at *Newsweek,* Richard Smith, Mark Whitaker and Jon Meacham. *Newsweek* is willing to devote tremendous resources and time to publishing this single important story. It is a legacy of commitment handed down from the late Katharine Graham and sustained and strengthened by her son Donald. This may be a first draft of history, as the late Phil Graham once described journalism, but it is so far the only thorough and penetrating account of one of the most interesting and important presidential elections in a long time.

Evan Thomas
November 22, 2004

INDEX

ABOUT THE AUTHORS

As ASSISTANT MANAGING EDITOR at *Newsweek* since April 1991, Evan Thomas has guided the magazine's overall coverage and written more than a hundred cover stories. He served as Washington bureau chief from 1986 to 1996 and is the author of the 1996 campaign chronicle, *Back from the Dead: How Clinton Survived the Republican Revolution*. He makes regular appearances on the "Today Show," "Meet the Press," "Charlie Rose," and "Imus in the Morning." His other books include *Robert Kennedy: His Life* and most recently the best-selling *John Paul Jones: Sailor, Hero, Father of the American Navy*.

Covering the Democrats are Eleanor Clift, one of Washington's best-known political reporters and a regular on "The McLaughlin Group," Jonathan Darman, a 2002 graduate of Harvard, and Suzanne Smalley, now a reporter at the *Boston Globe*. Covering the Republicans is Kevin Peraino, who most recently reported the invasion of Iraq with the Third Infantry Division. Coordinating the coverage is Peter Goldman, longtime senior writer at *Newsweek*.

PUBLICAFFAIRS is a publishing house founded in 1997. It is a tribute to the standards, values, and flair of three persons who have served as mentors to countless reporters, writers, editors, and book people of all kinds, including me.

I. F. STONE, proprietor of *I. F. Stone's Weekly,* combined a commitment to the First Amendment with entrepreneurial zeal and reporting skill and became one of the great independent journalists in American history. At the age of eighty, Izzy published *The Trial of Socrates,* which was a national bestseller. He wrote the book after he taught himself ancient Greek.

BENJAMIN C. BRADLEE was for nearly thirty years the charismatic editorial leader of *The Washington Post.* It was Ben who gave the *Post* the range and courage to pursue such historic issues as Watergate. He supported his reporters with a tenacity that made them fearless, and it is no accident that so many became authors of influential, best-selling books.

ROBERT L. BERNSTEIN, the chief executive of Random House for more than a quarter century, guided one of the nation's premier publishing houses. Bob was personally responsible for many books of political dissent and argument that challenged tyranny around the globe. He is also the founder and was the longtime chair of Human Rights Watch, one of the most respected human rights organizations in the world.

.   .   .

For fifty years, the banner of Public Affairs Press was carried by its owner Morris B. Schnapper, who published Gandhi, Nasser, Toynbee, Truman, and about 1,500 other authors. In 1983 Schnapper was described by *The Washington Post* as "a redoubtable gadfly." His legacy will endure in the books to come.

Peter Osnos, *Publisher*